Youthful Colouring

By

Lynda K Miller
© 2020

www.lyndasart.weebly.com

The designs are on the front of the pages only, nice and bold, ideal for experimental colouring

For all ages to enjoy the process of colouring

You might want to put a piece of card between the pages when colouring in to keep the next one clean

As always special thanks to Croggy, my number one fan

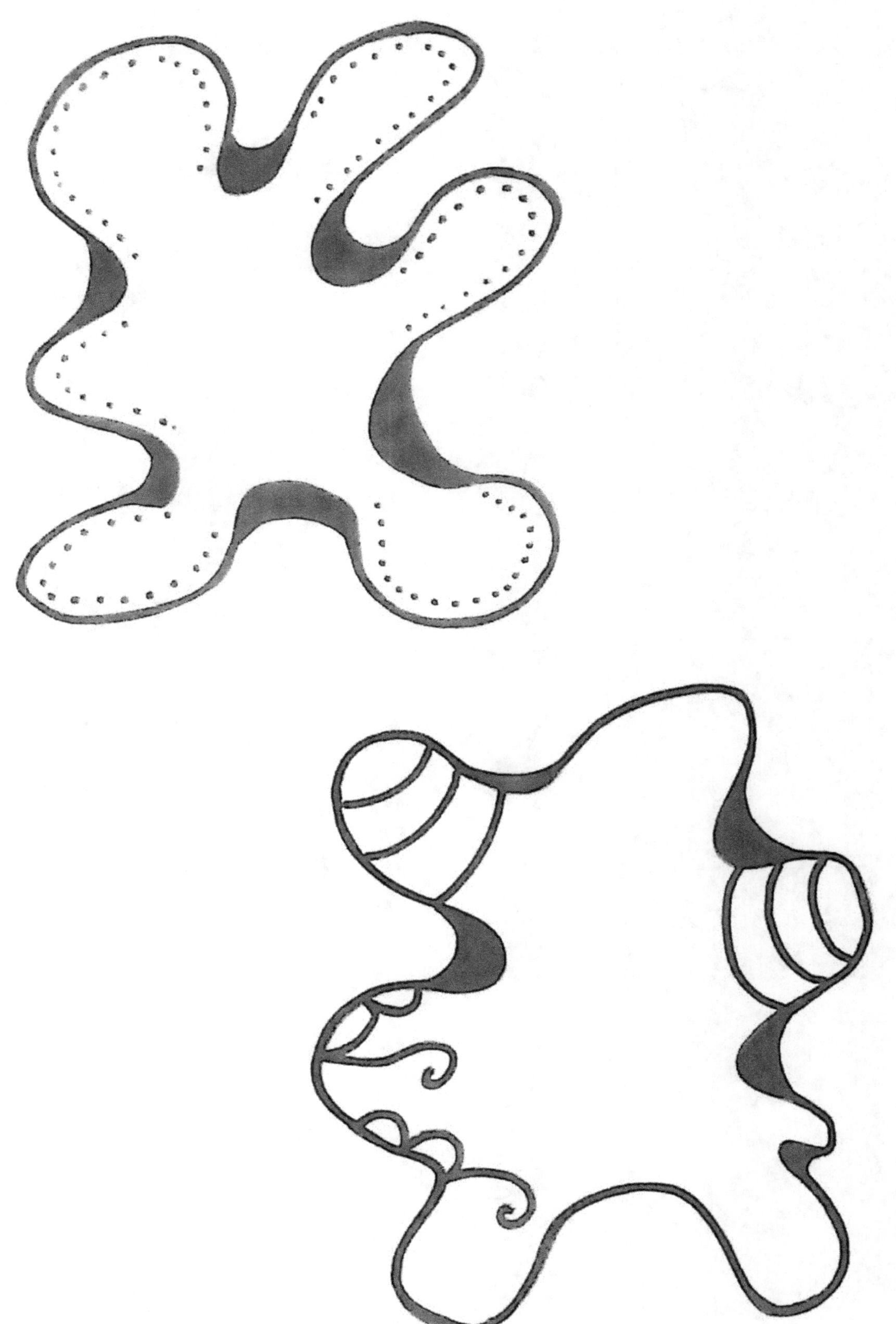

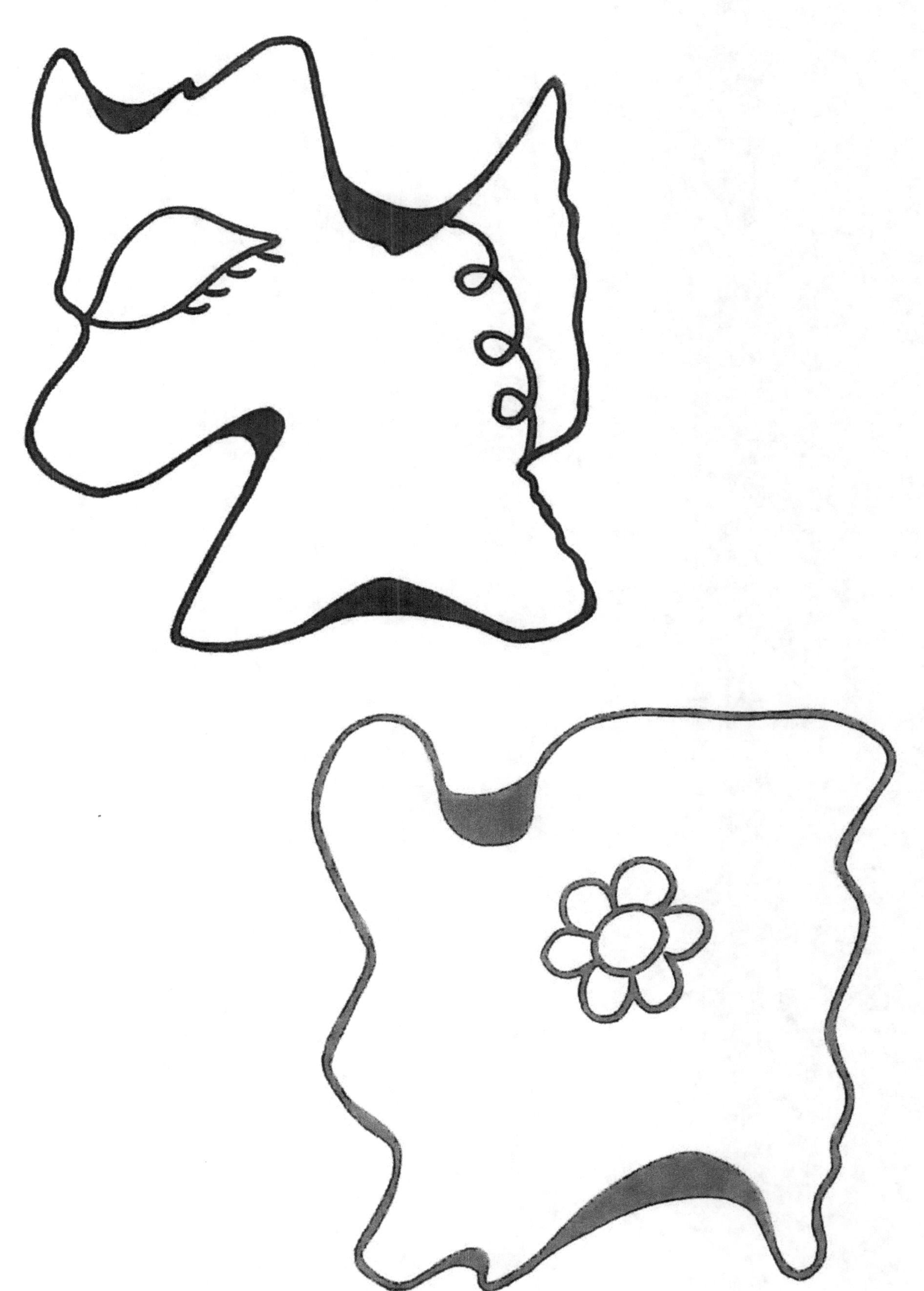

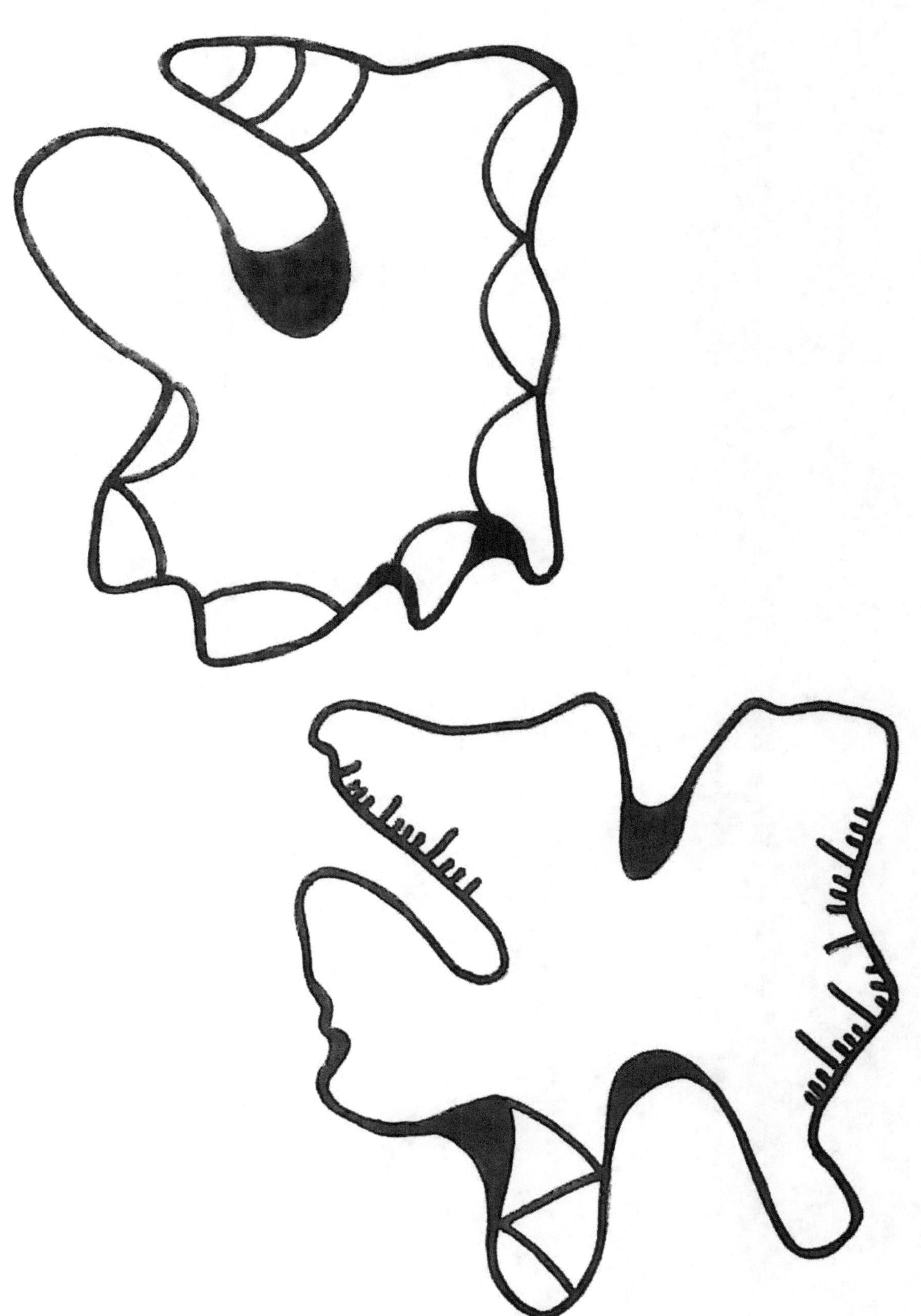

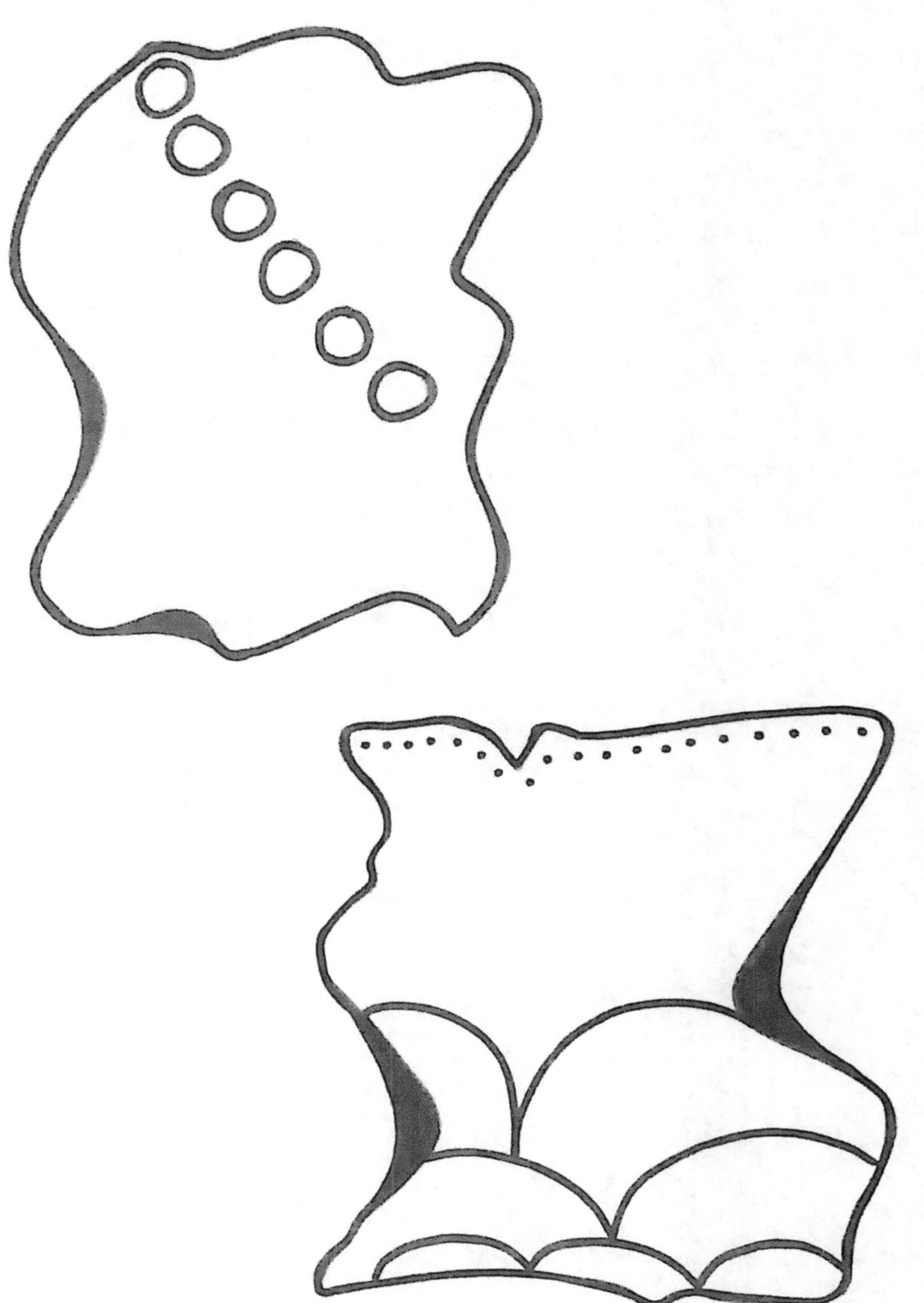

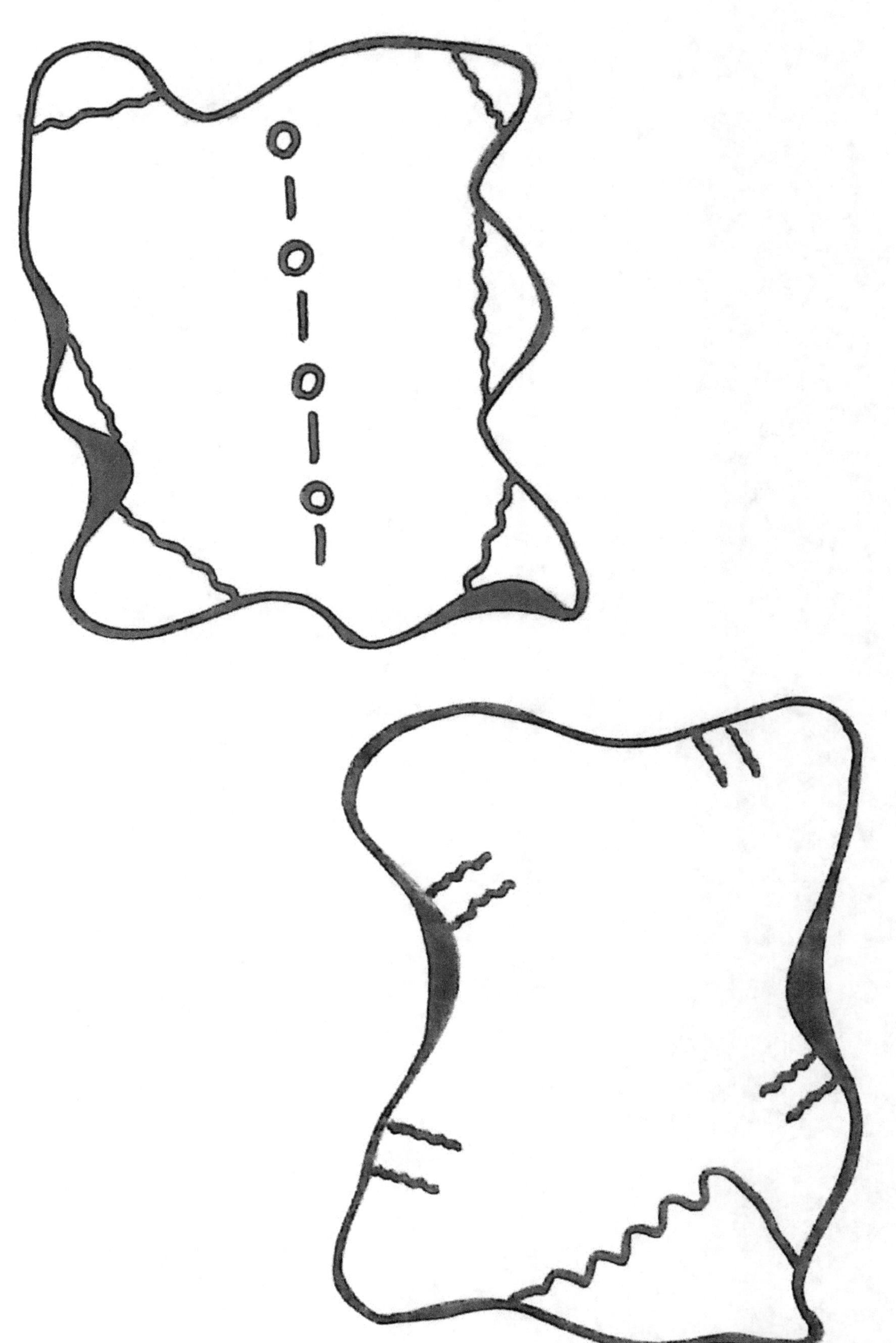

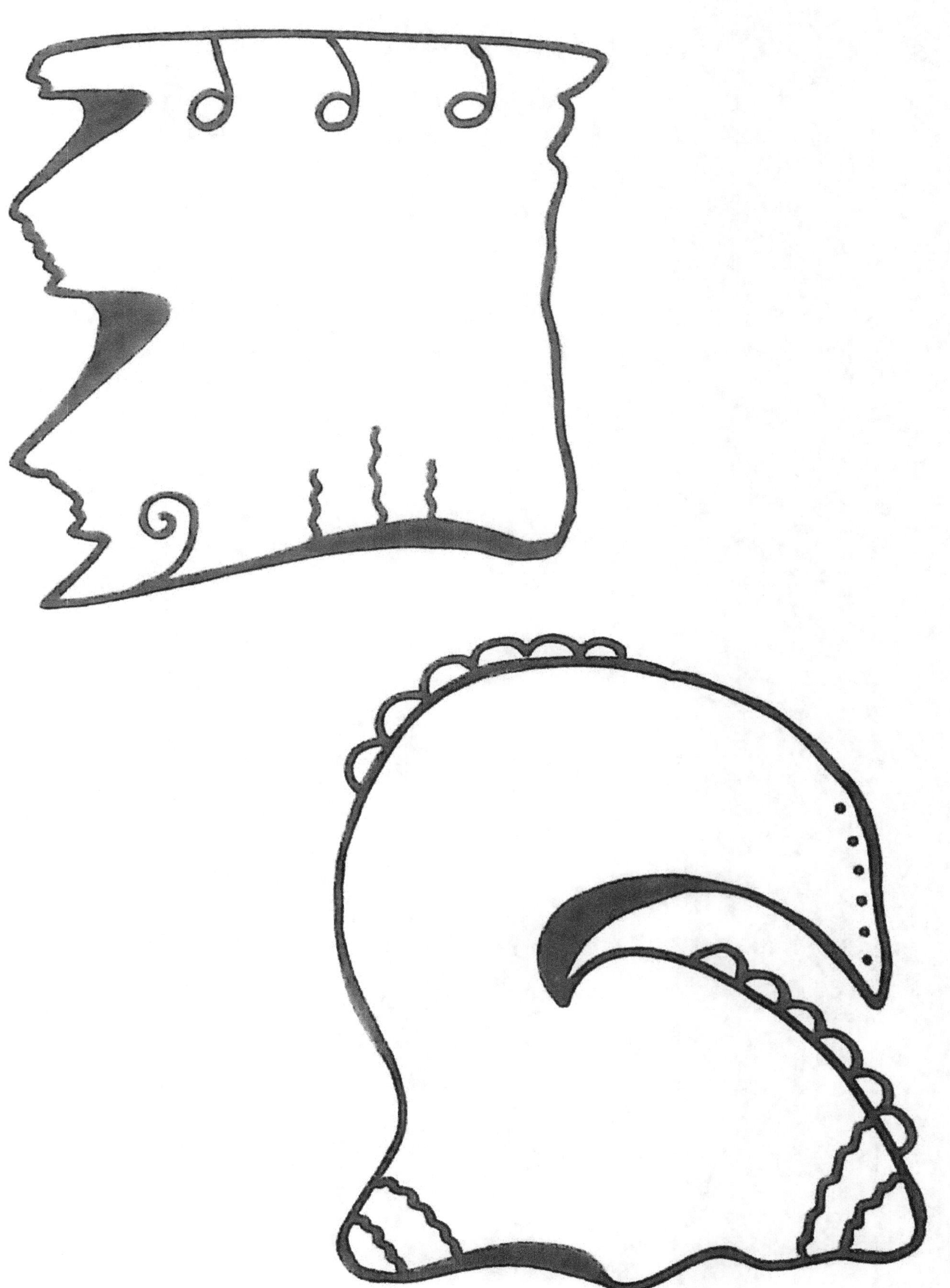

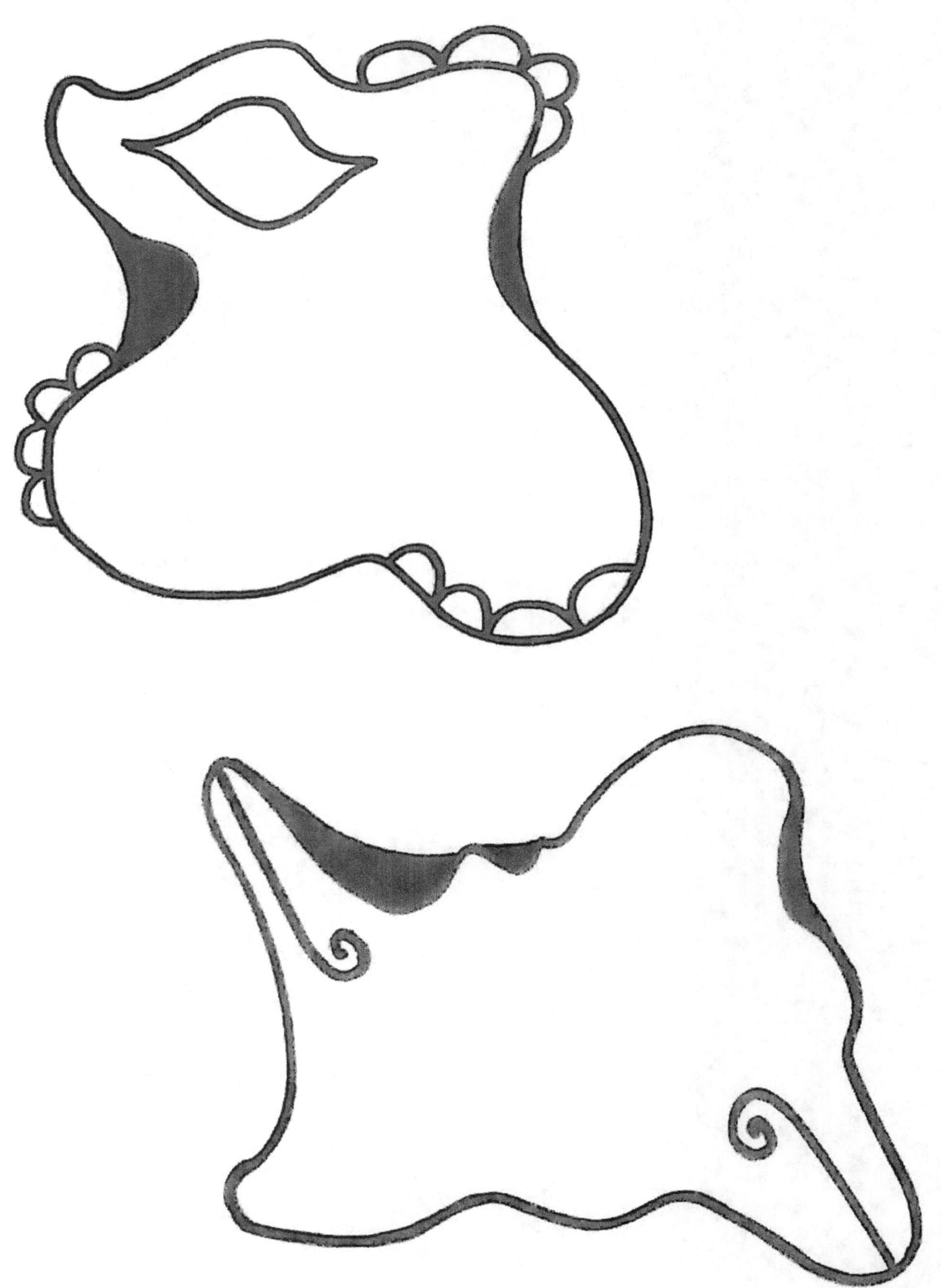

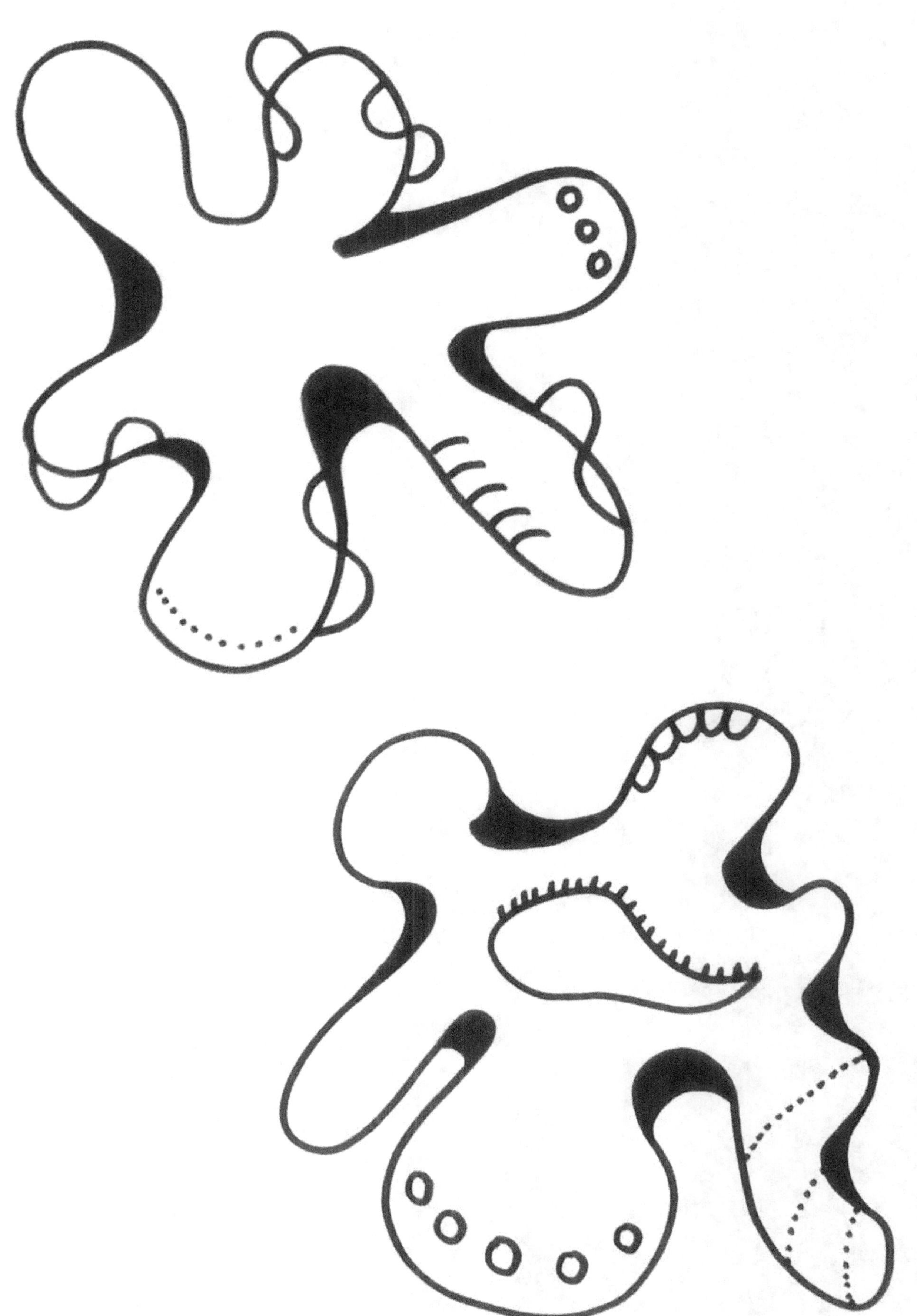

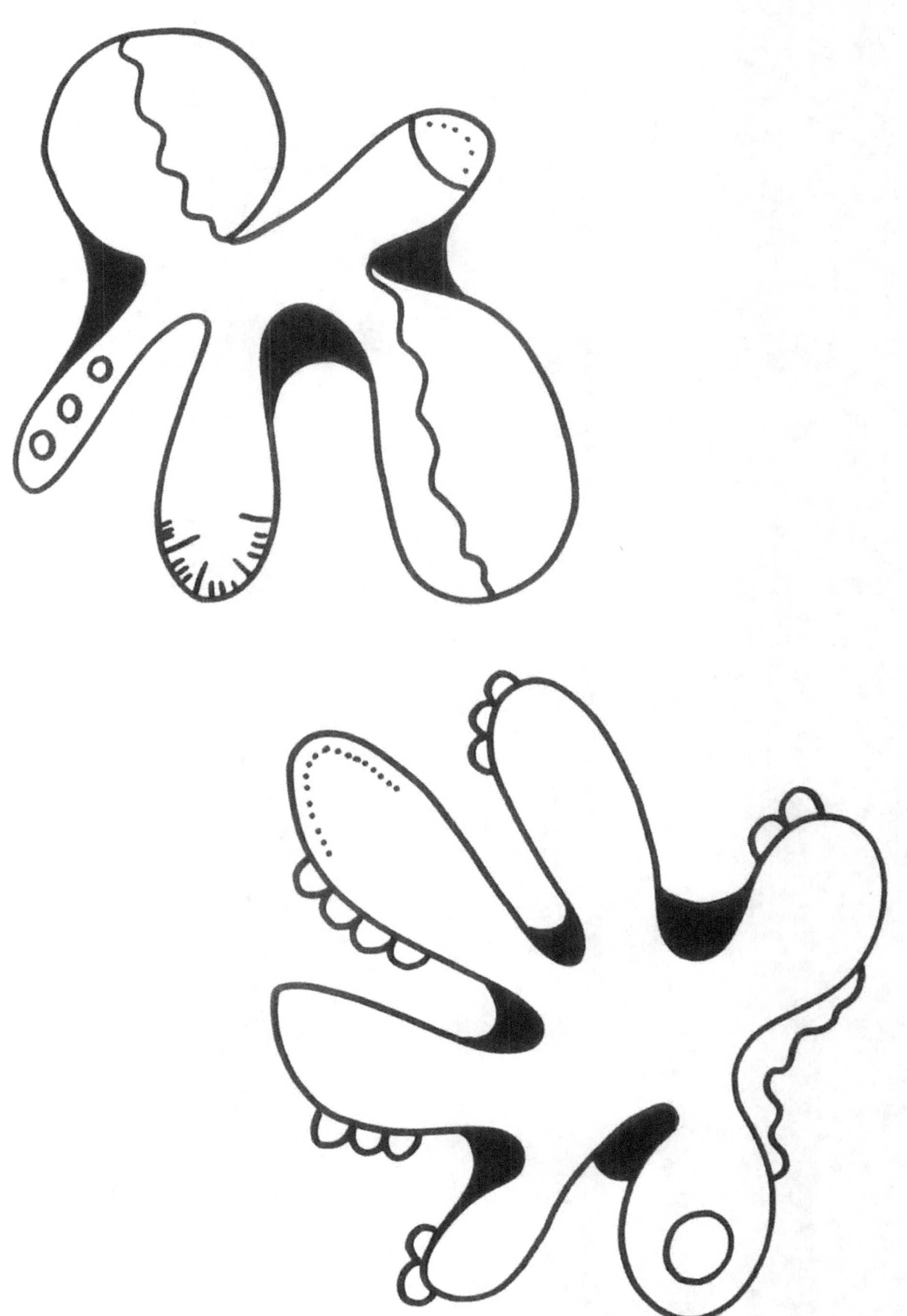

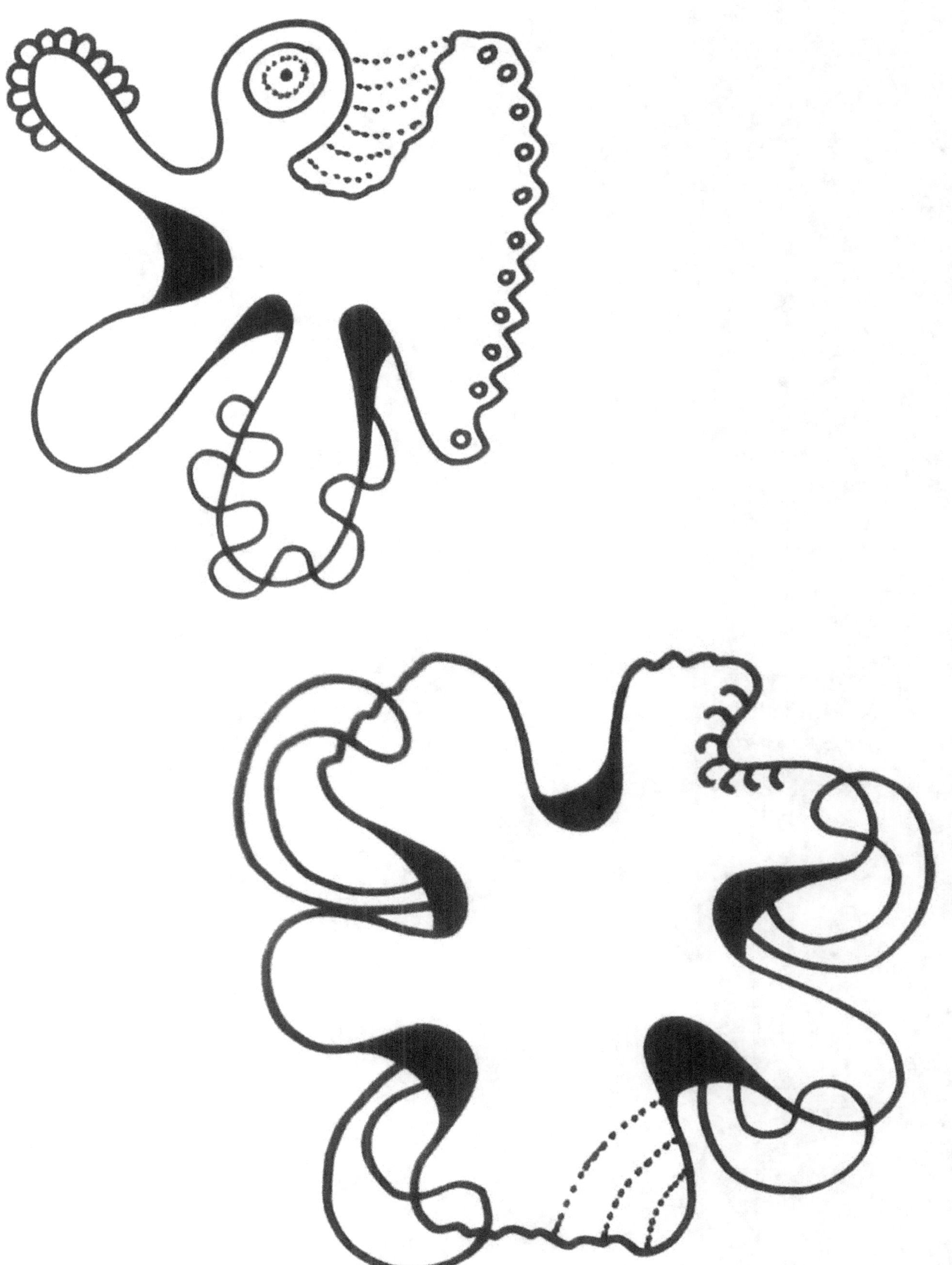

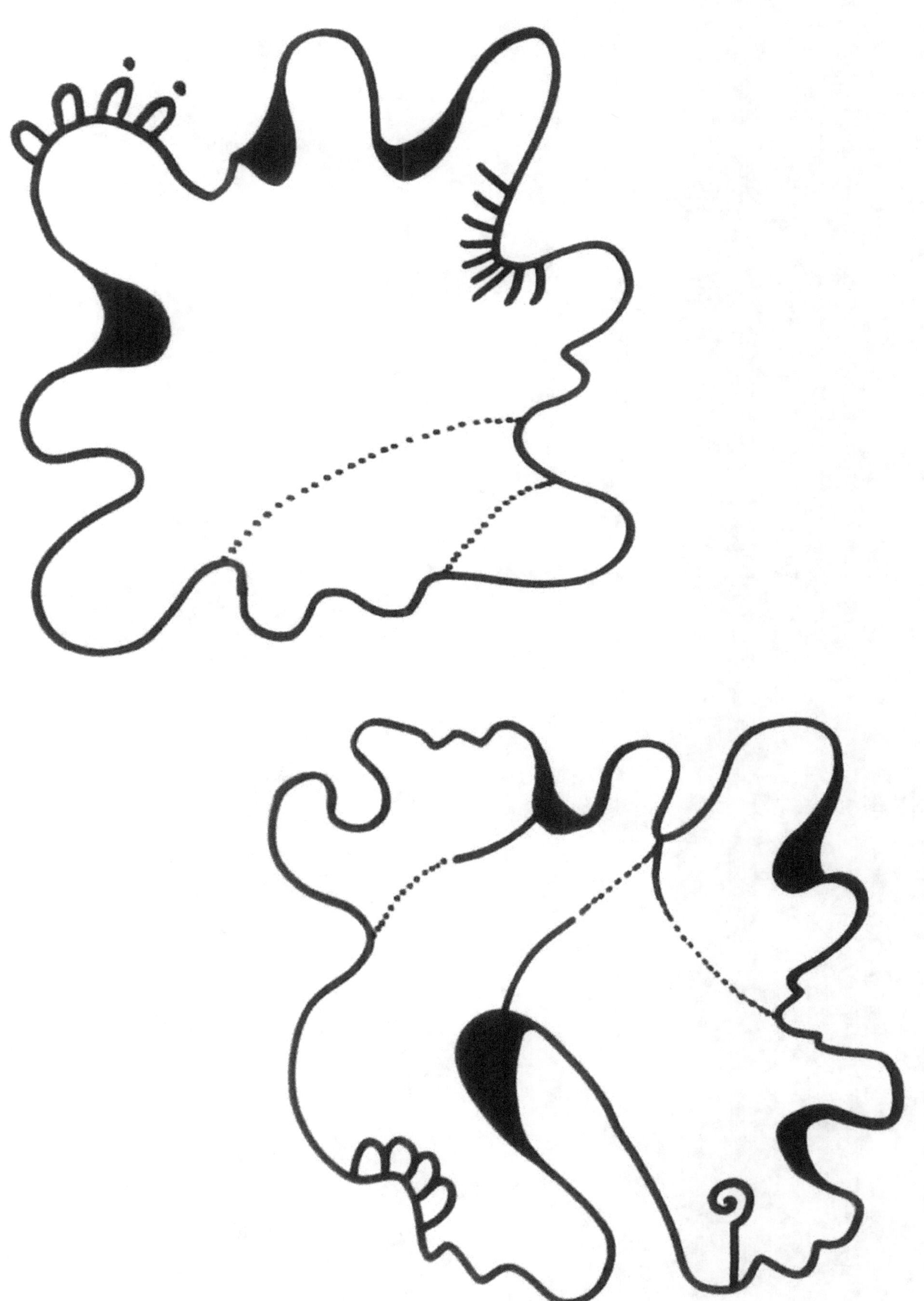

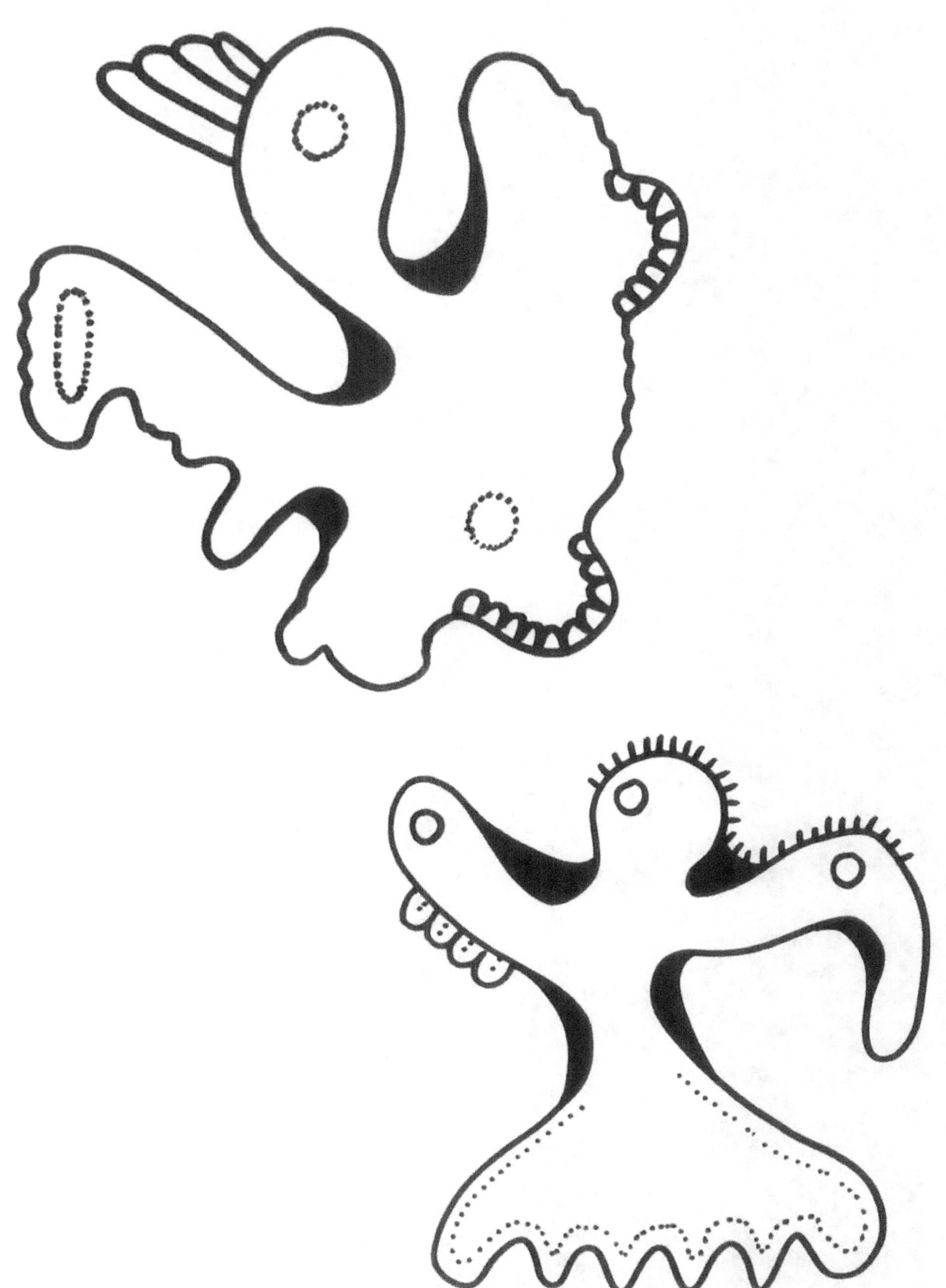

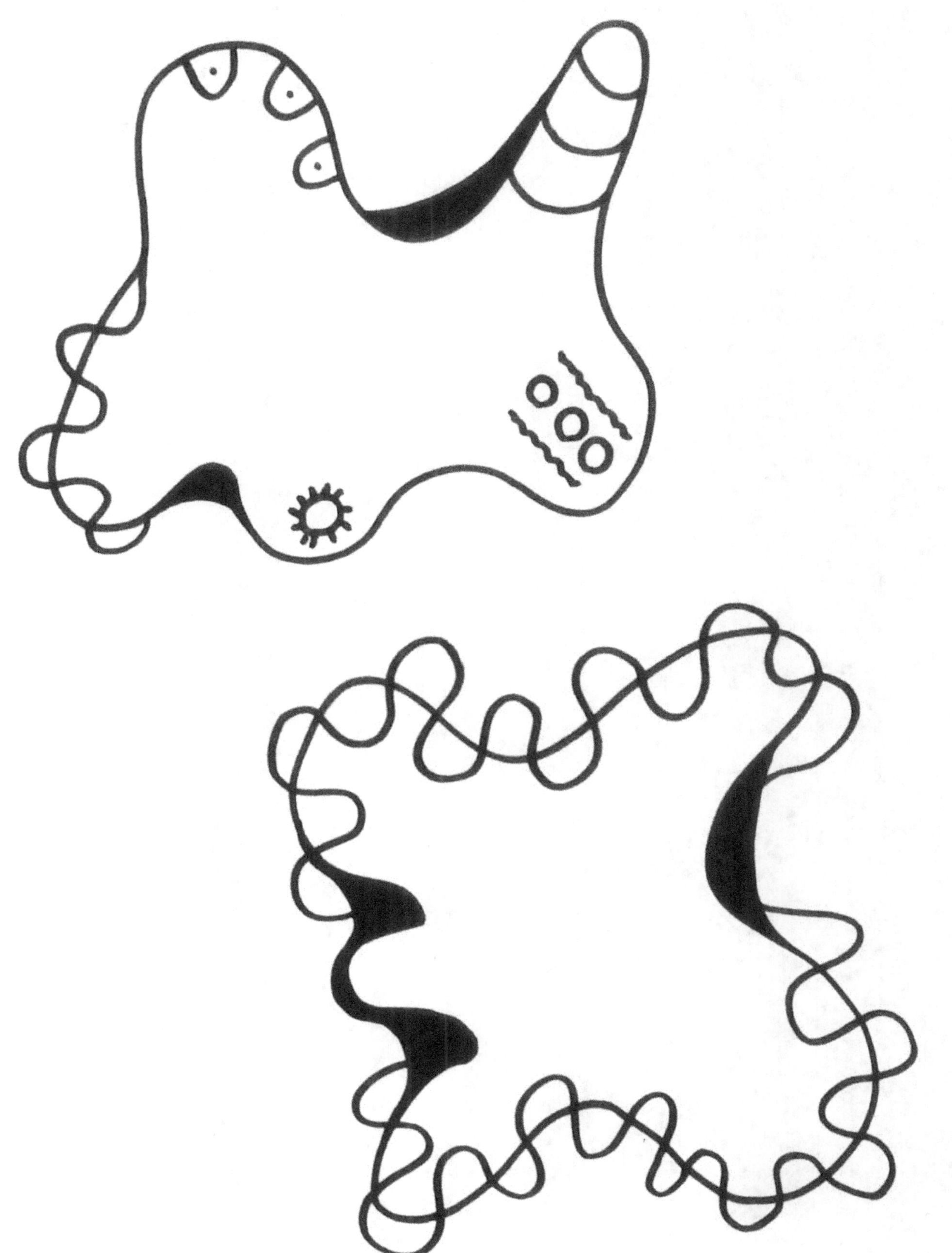

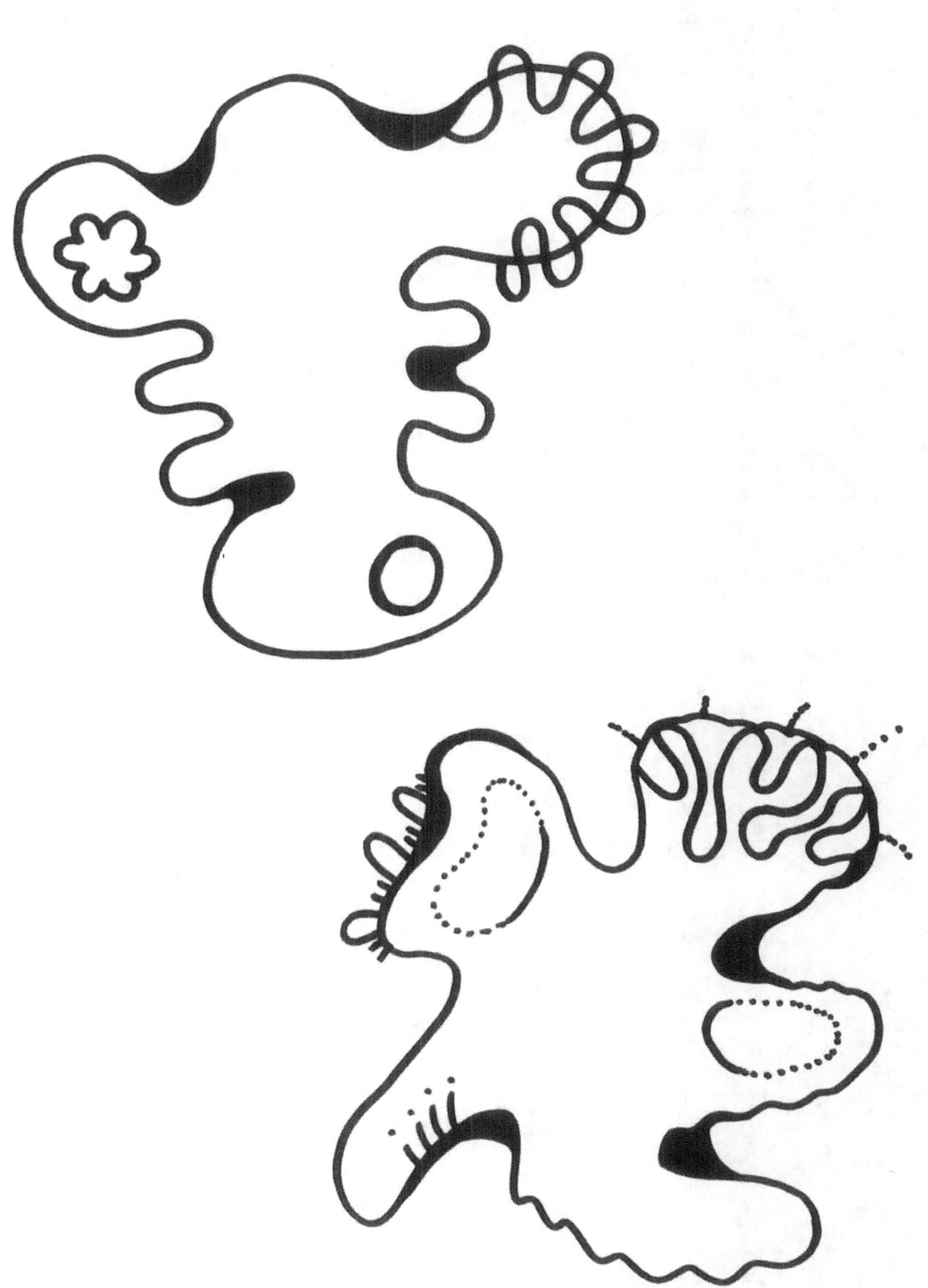

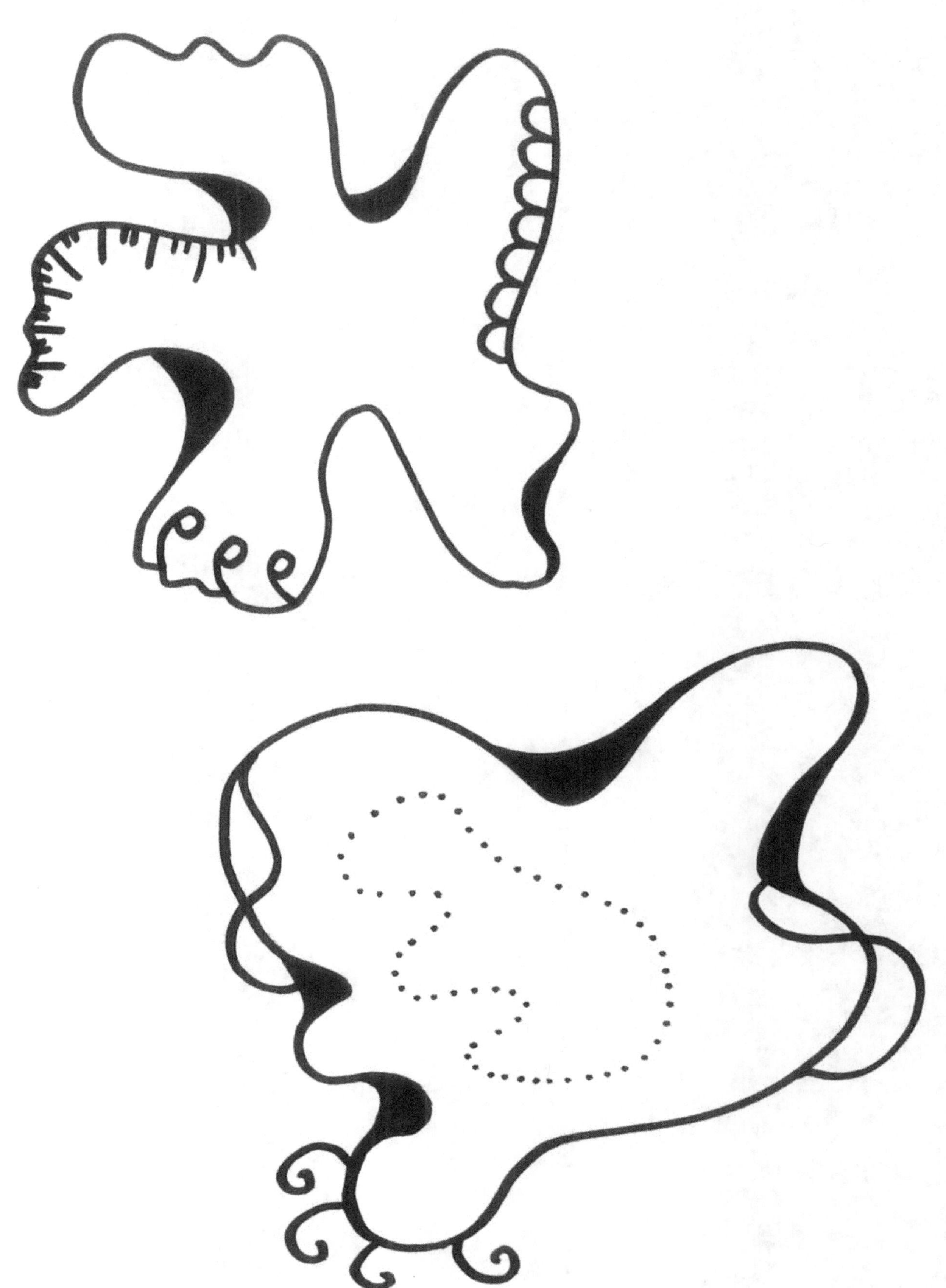

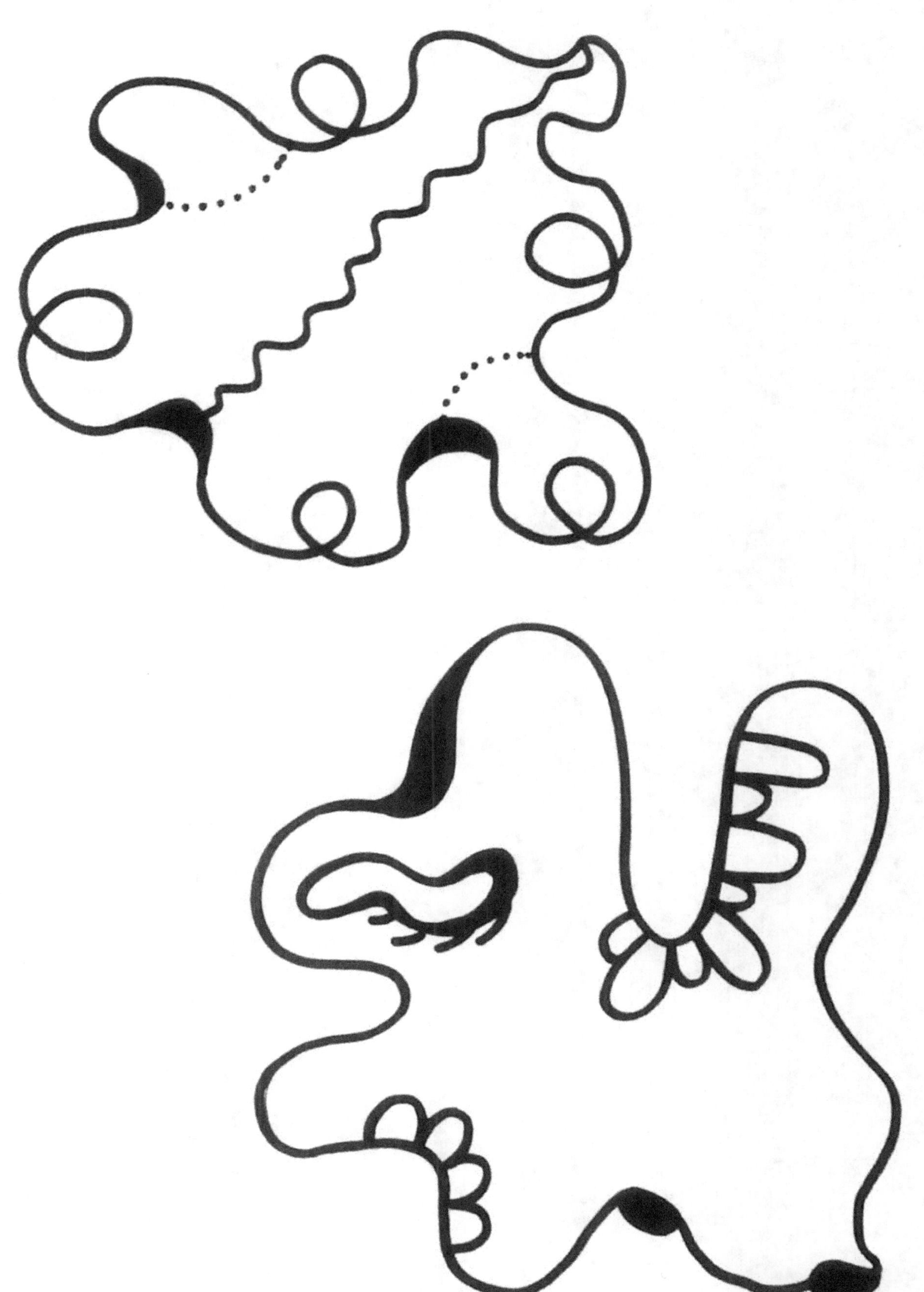

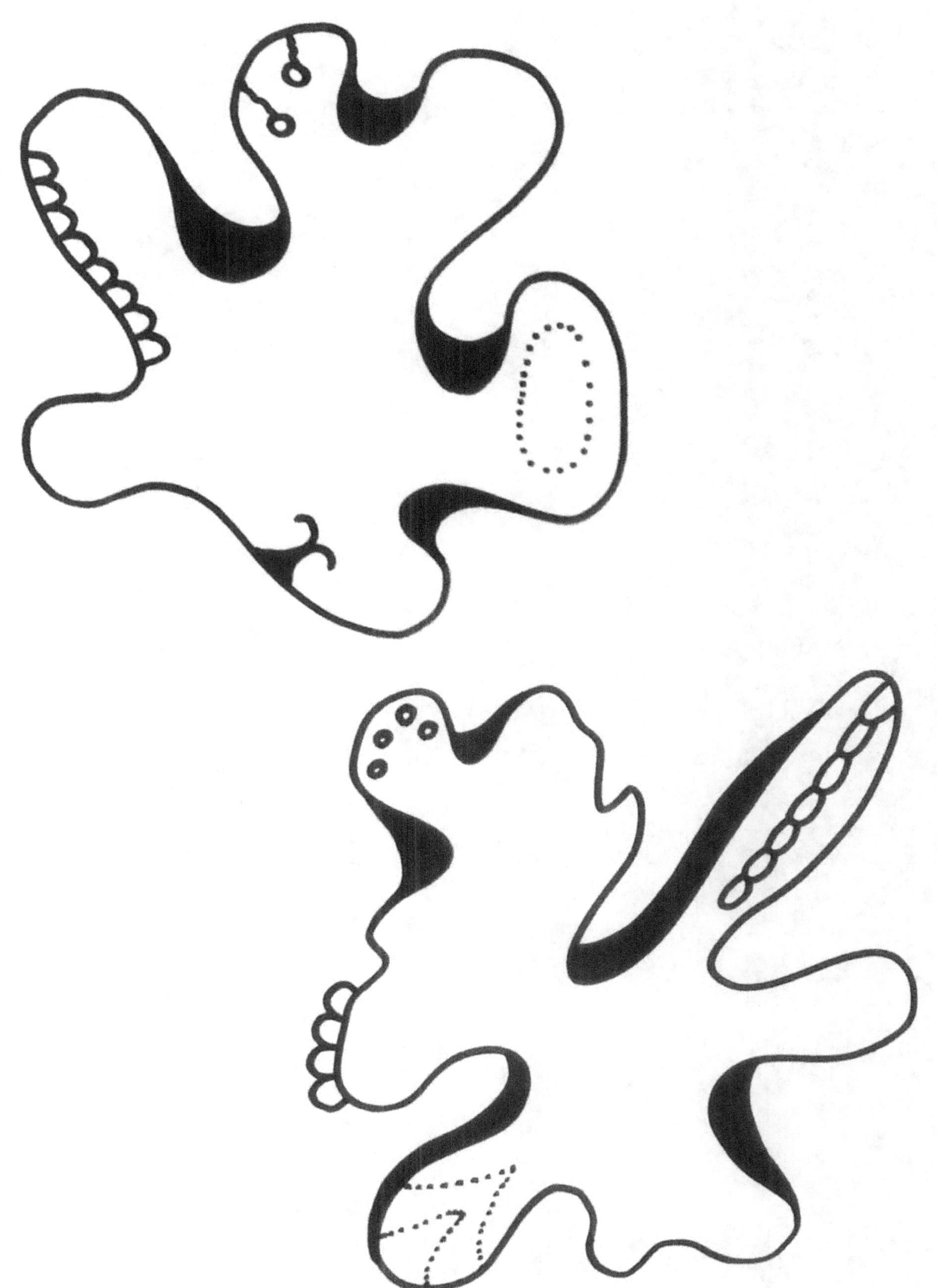

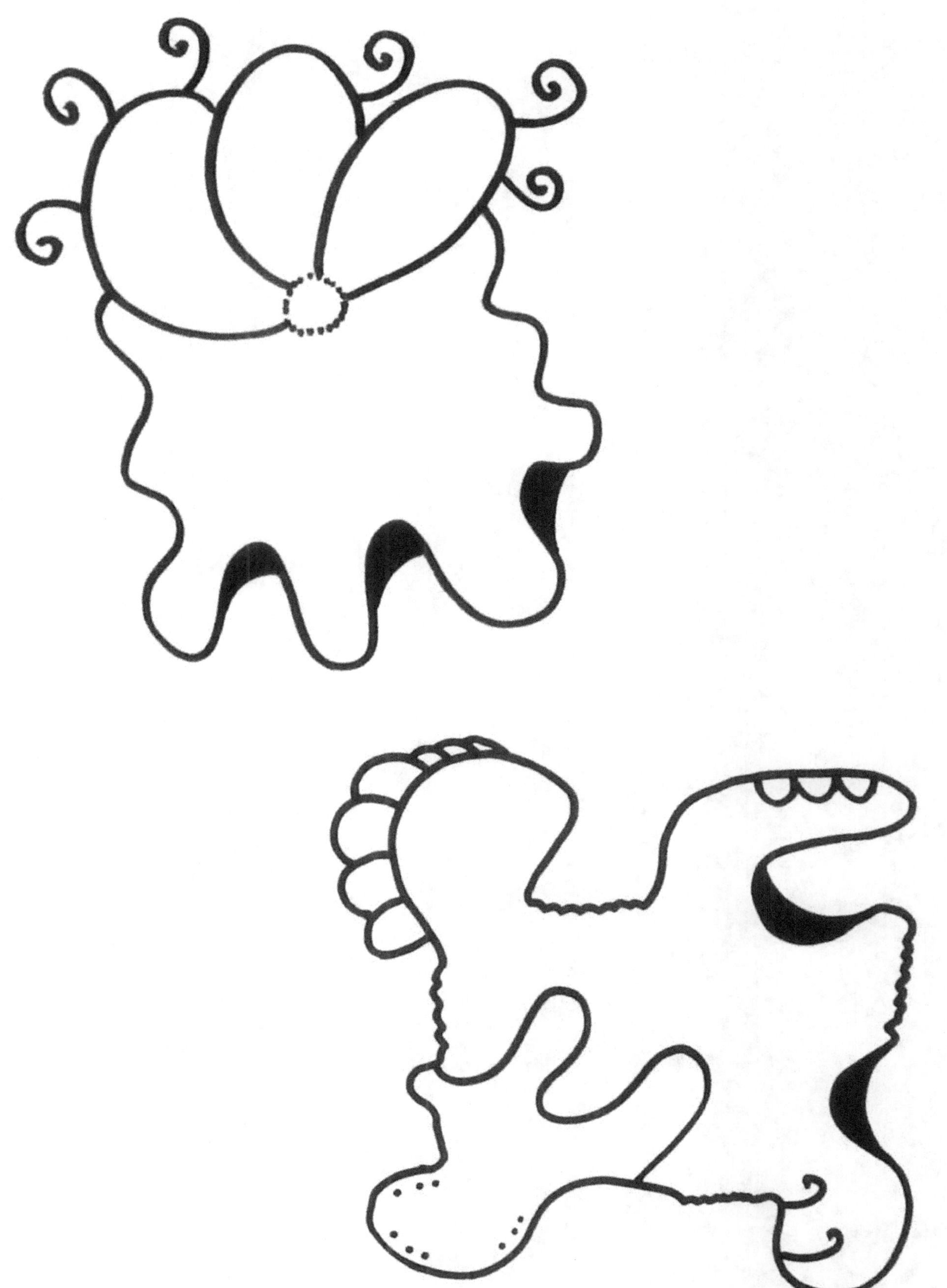

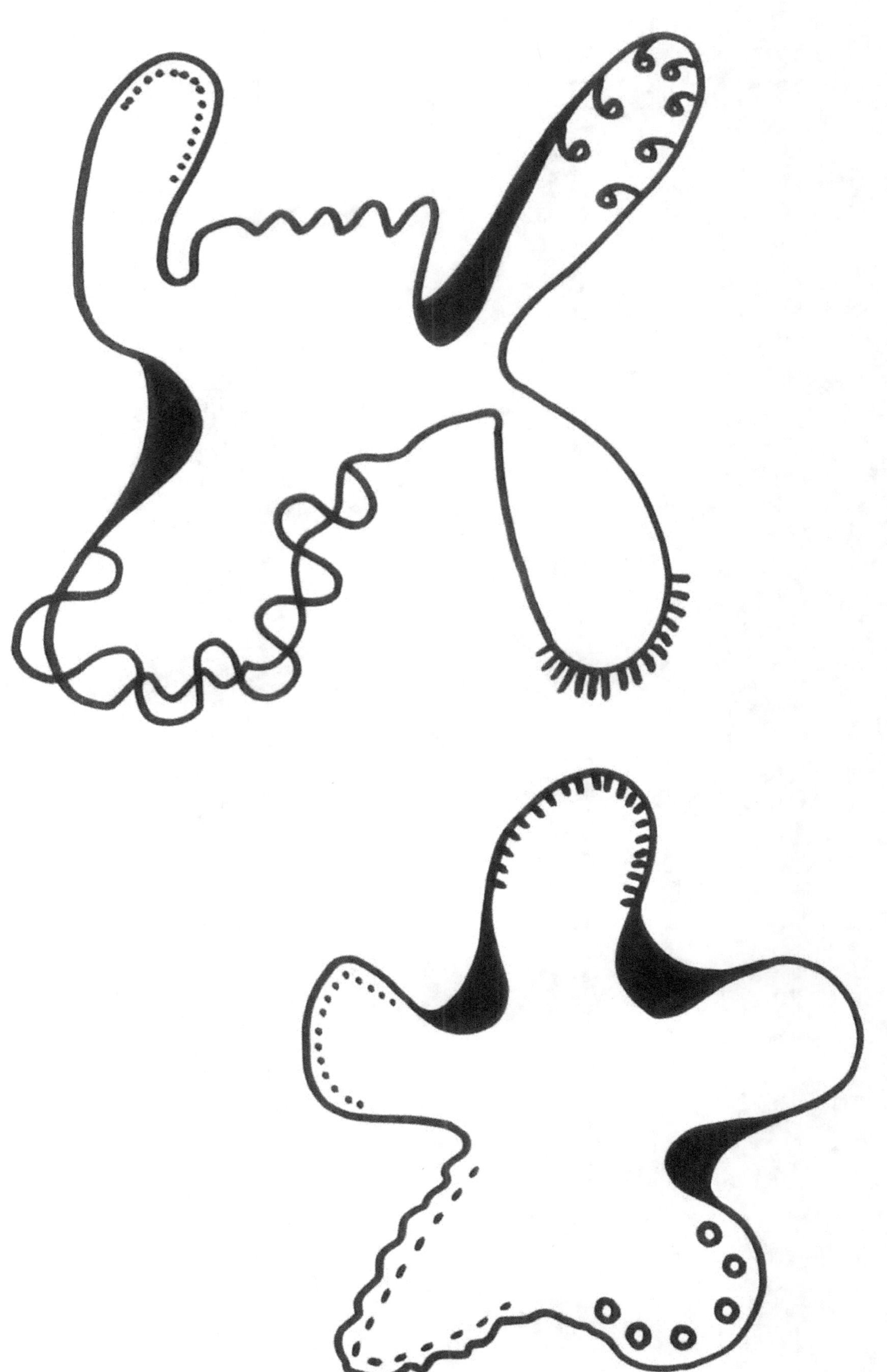

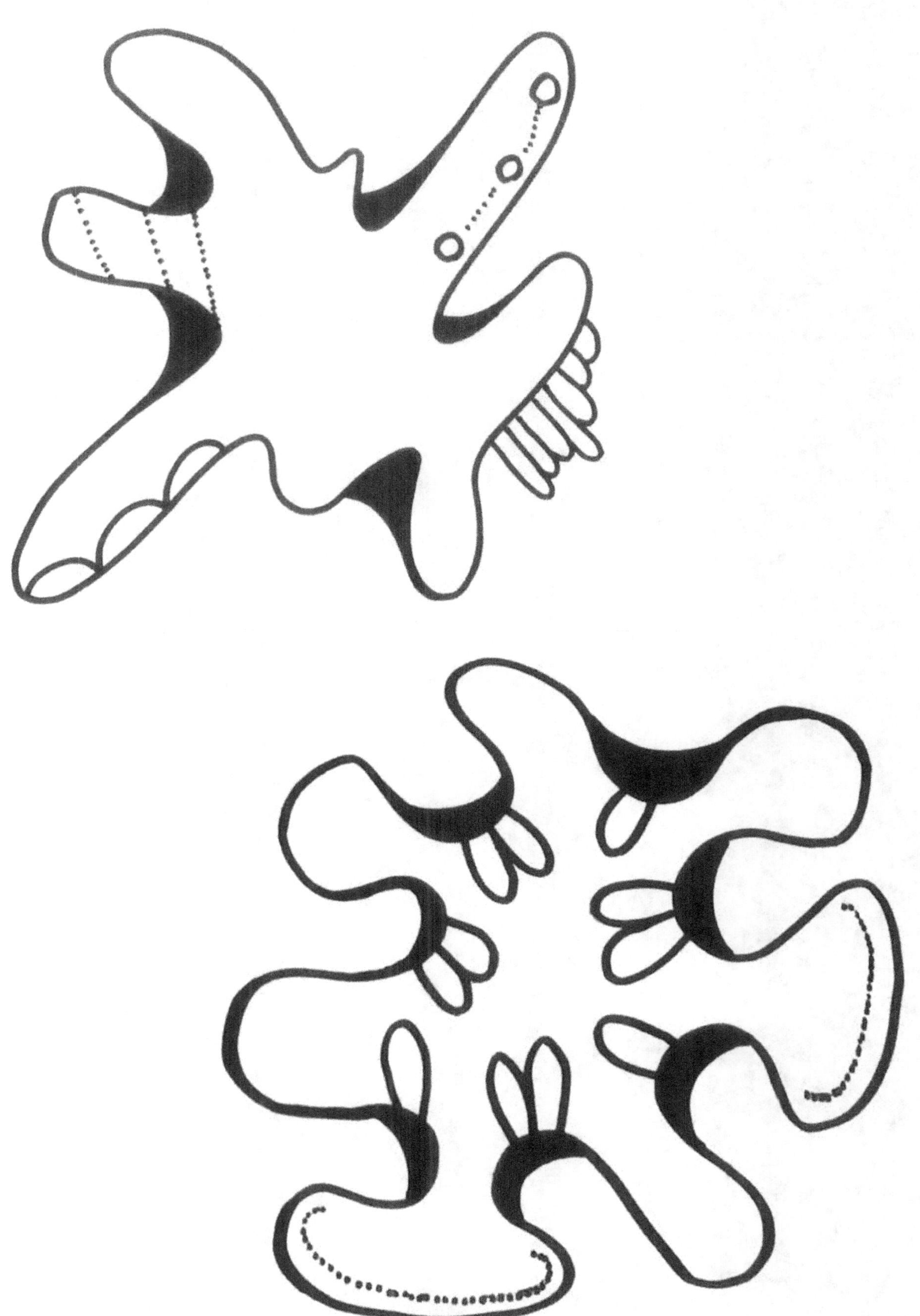

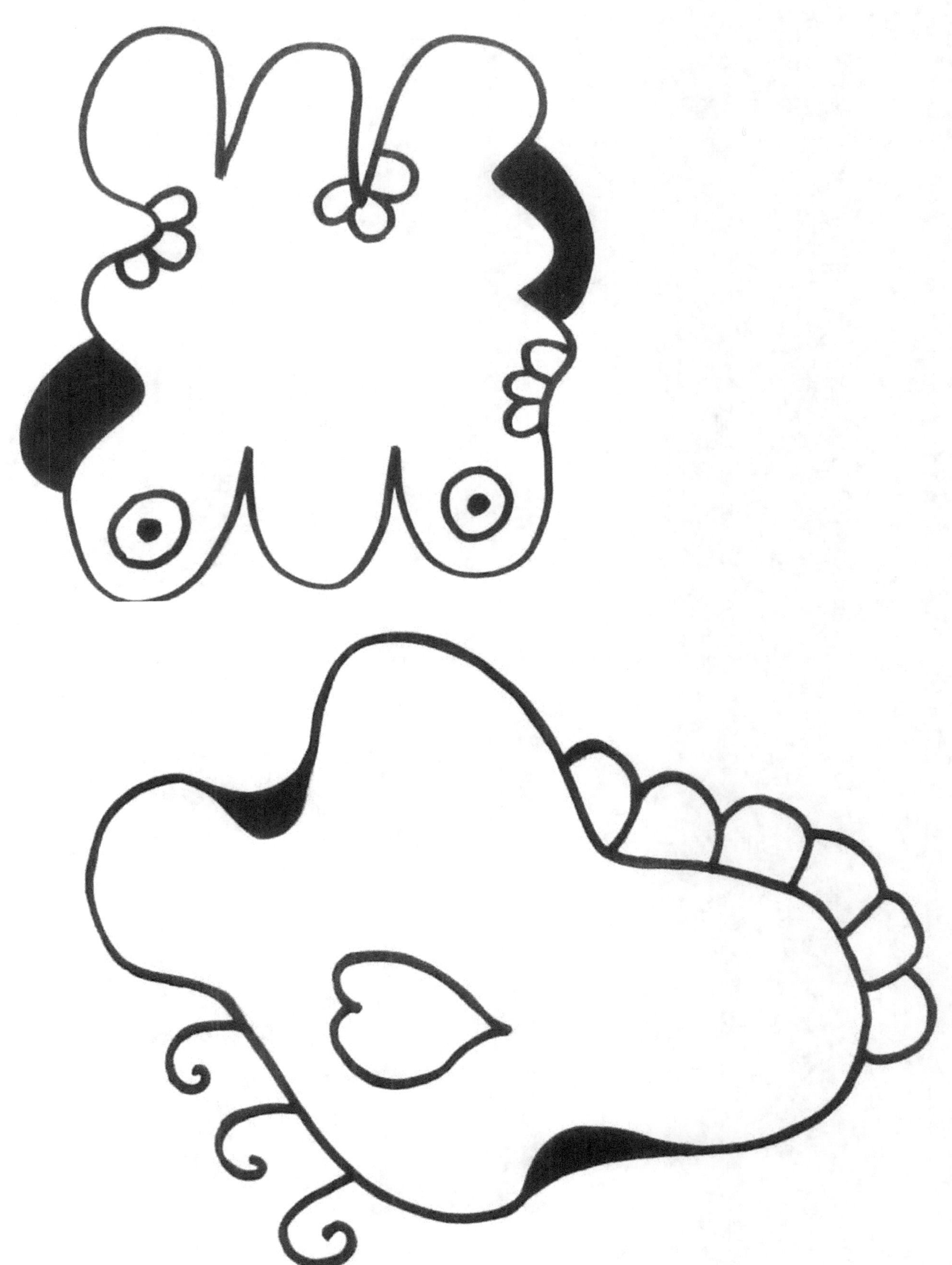

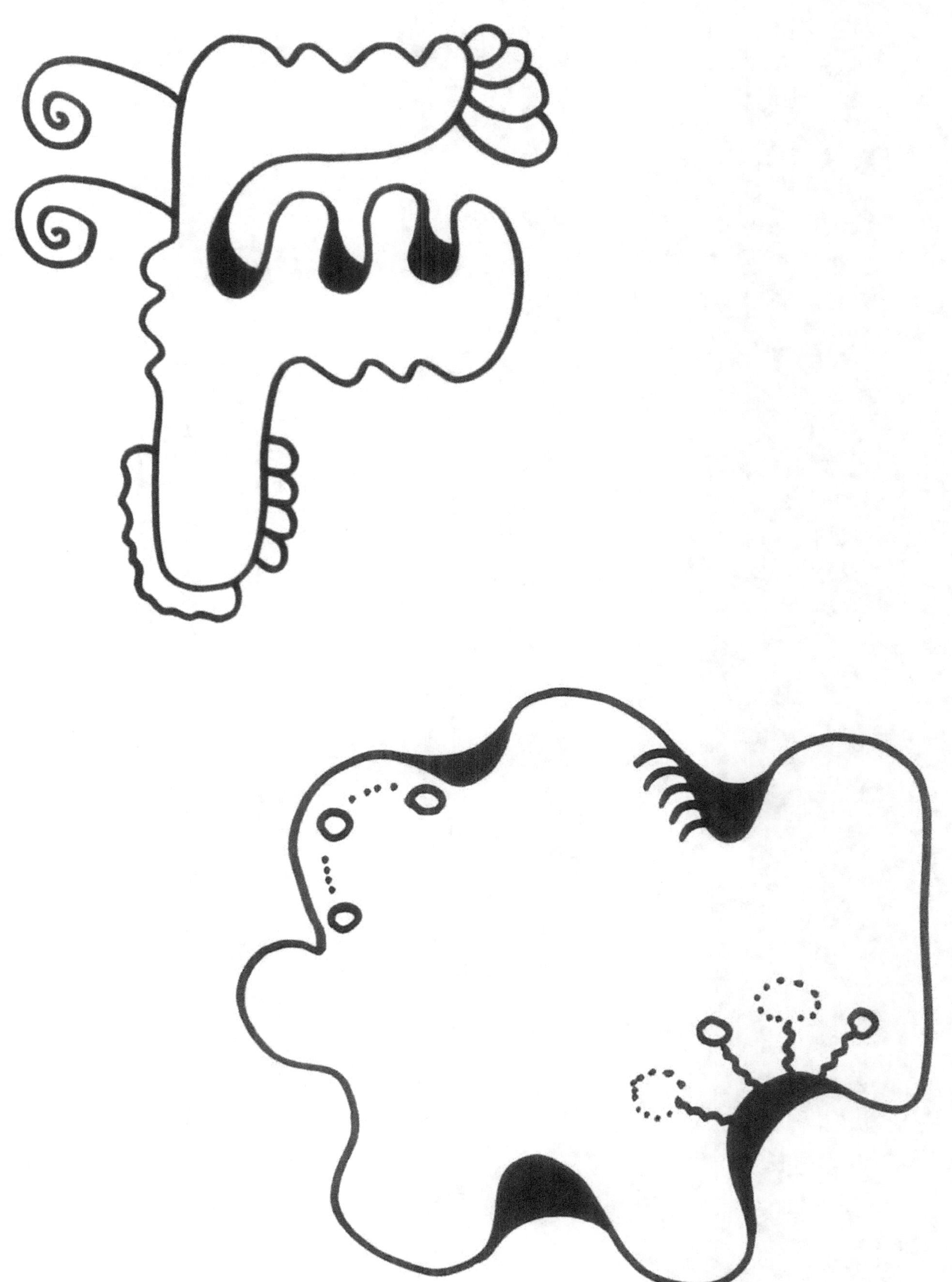

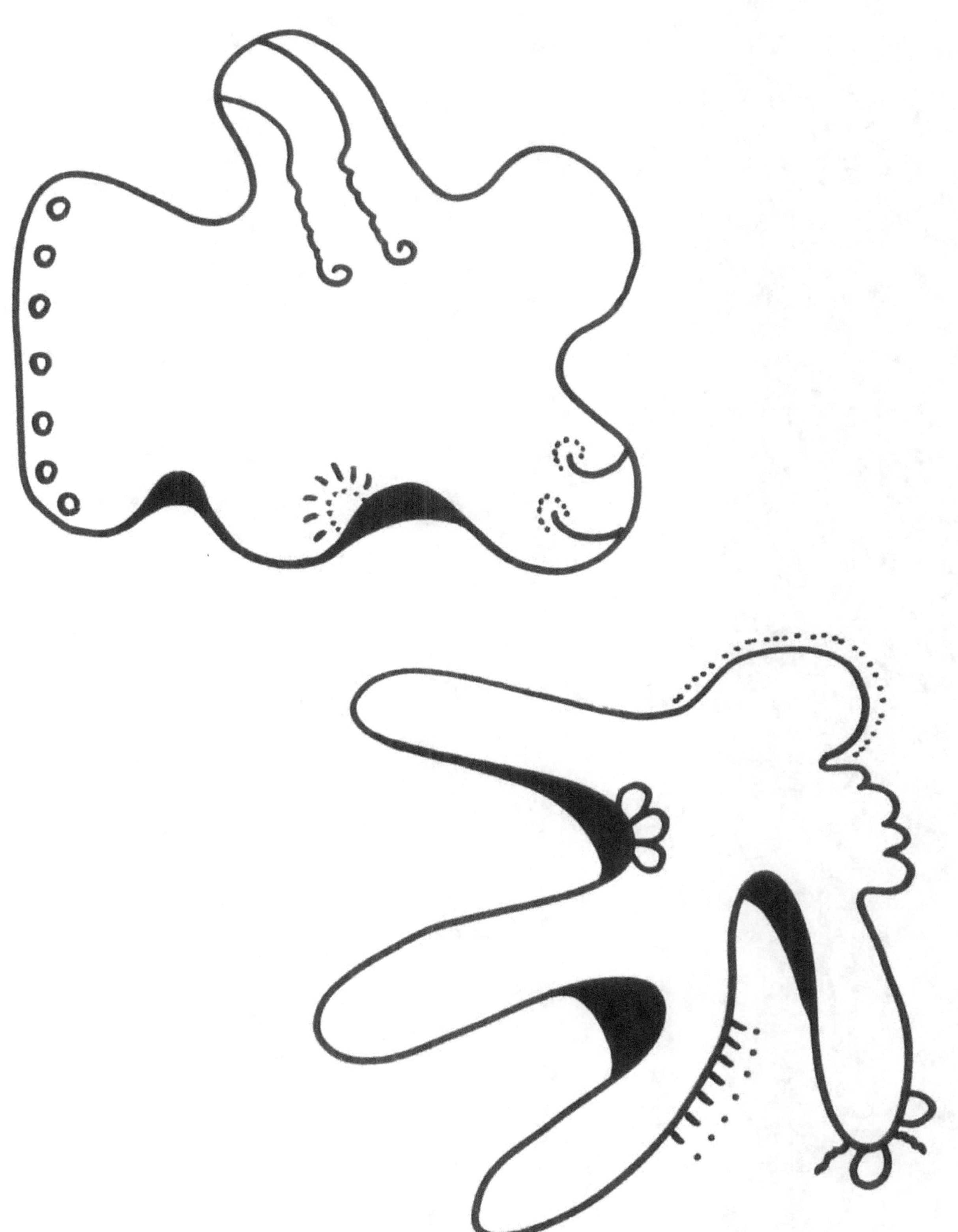

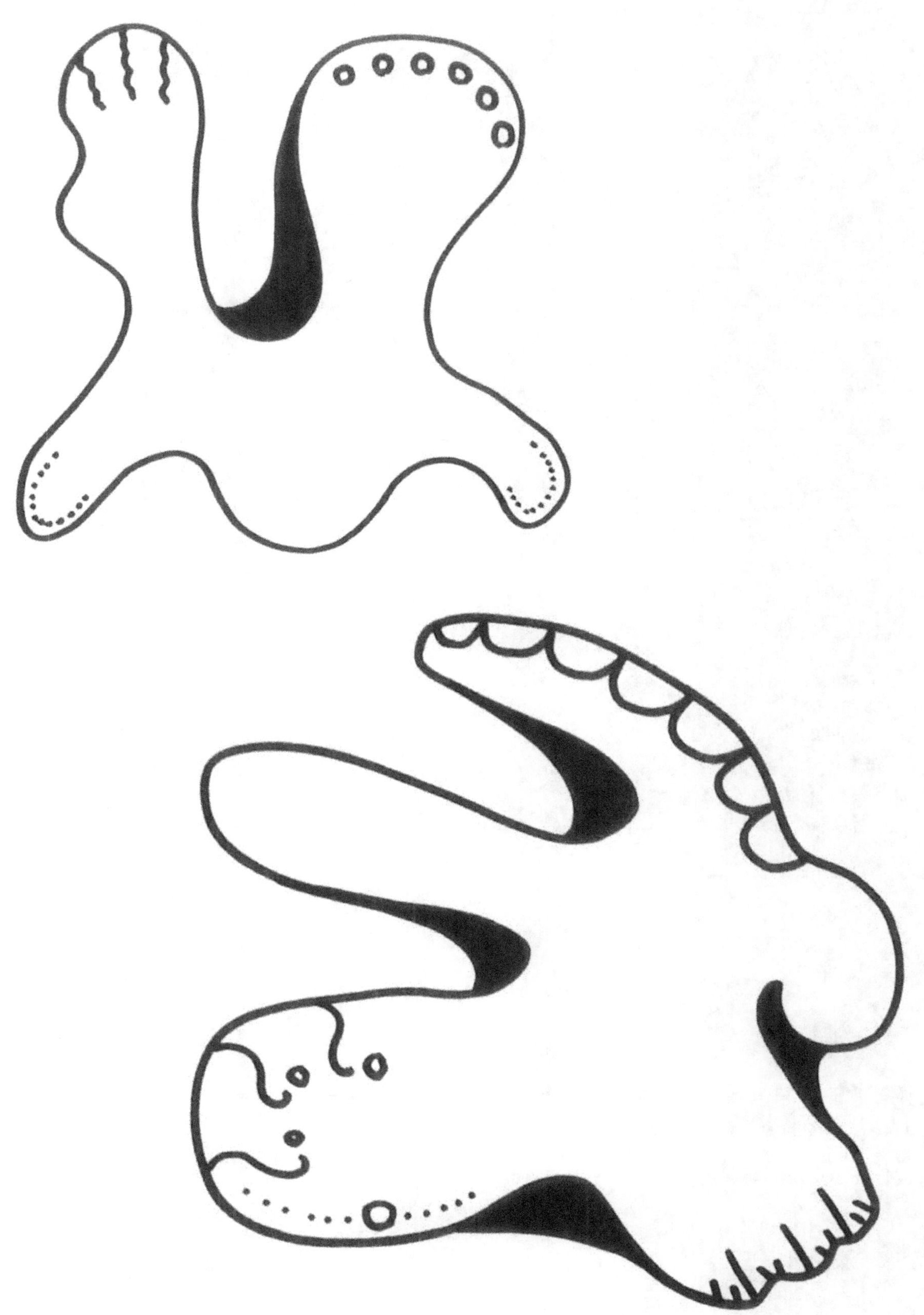

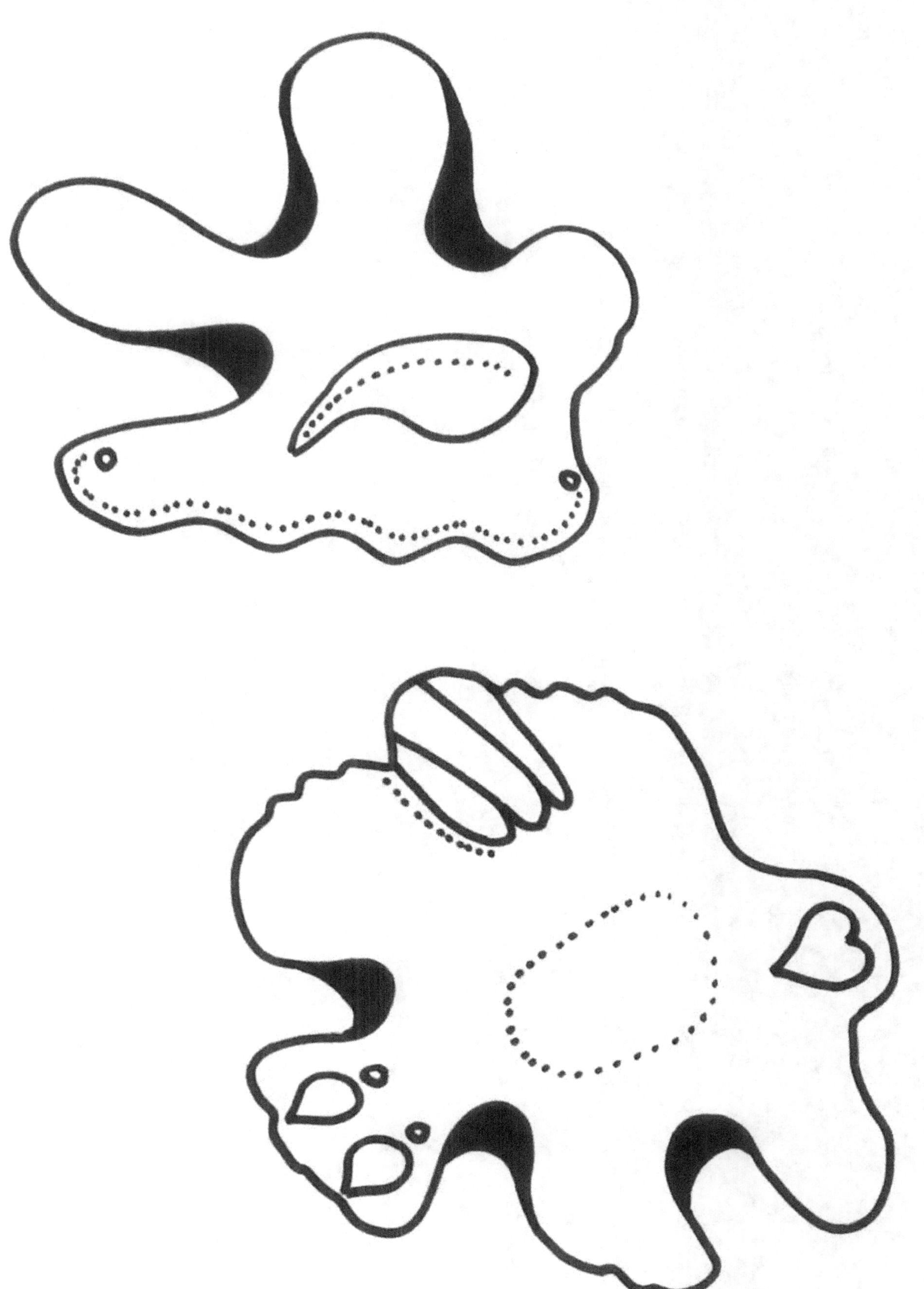

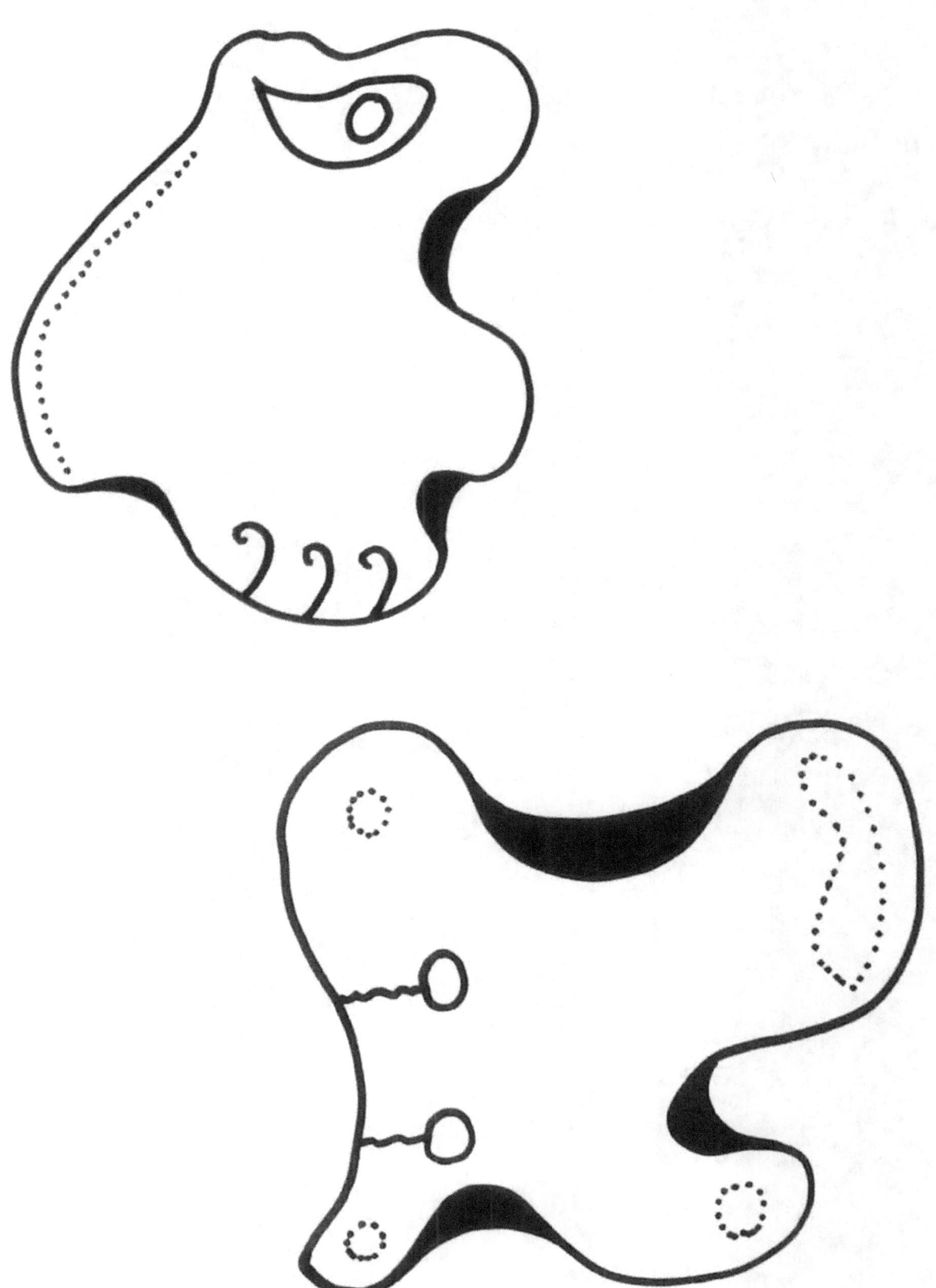

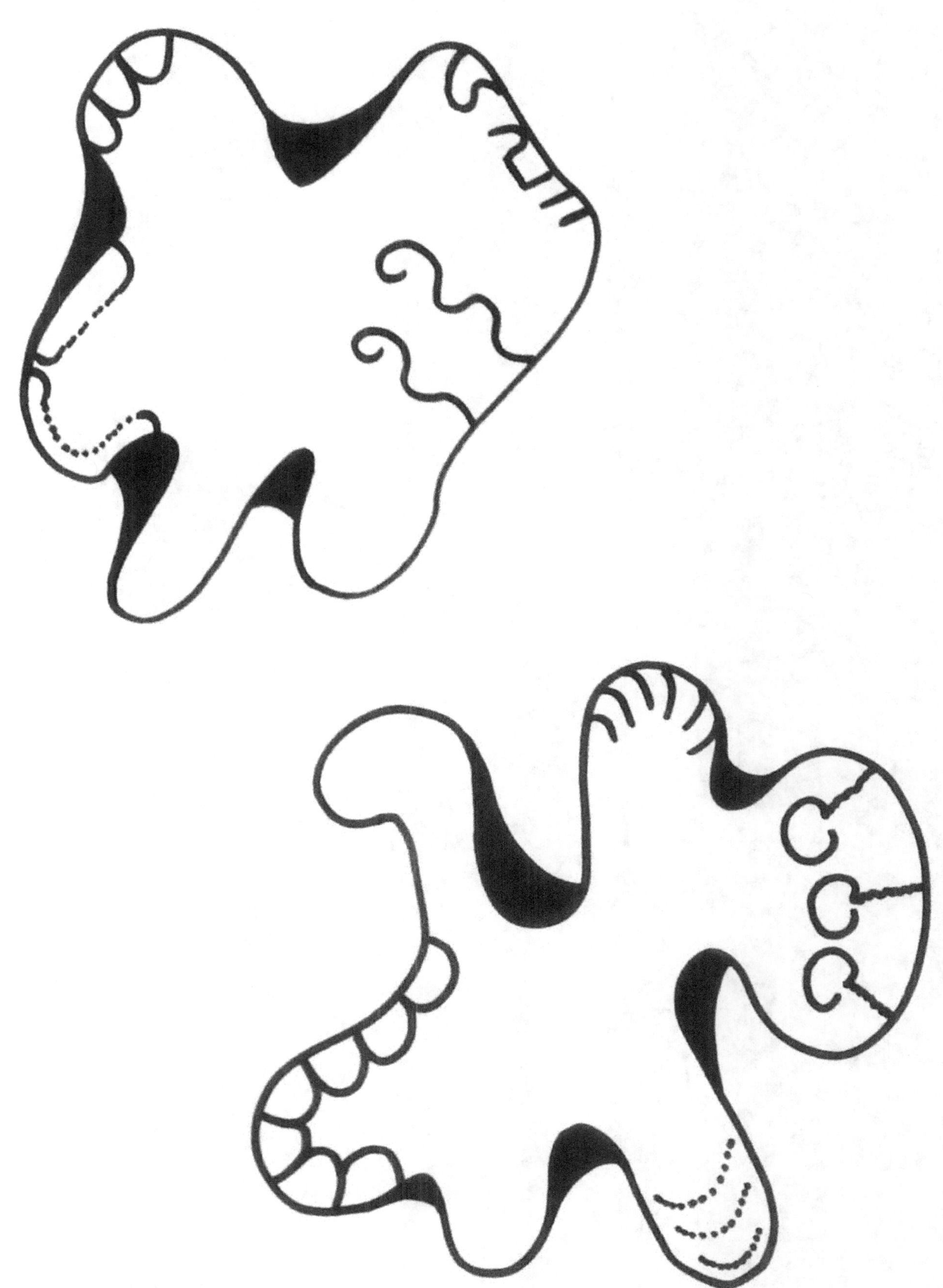

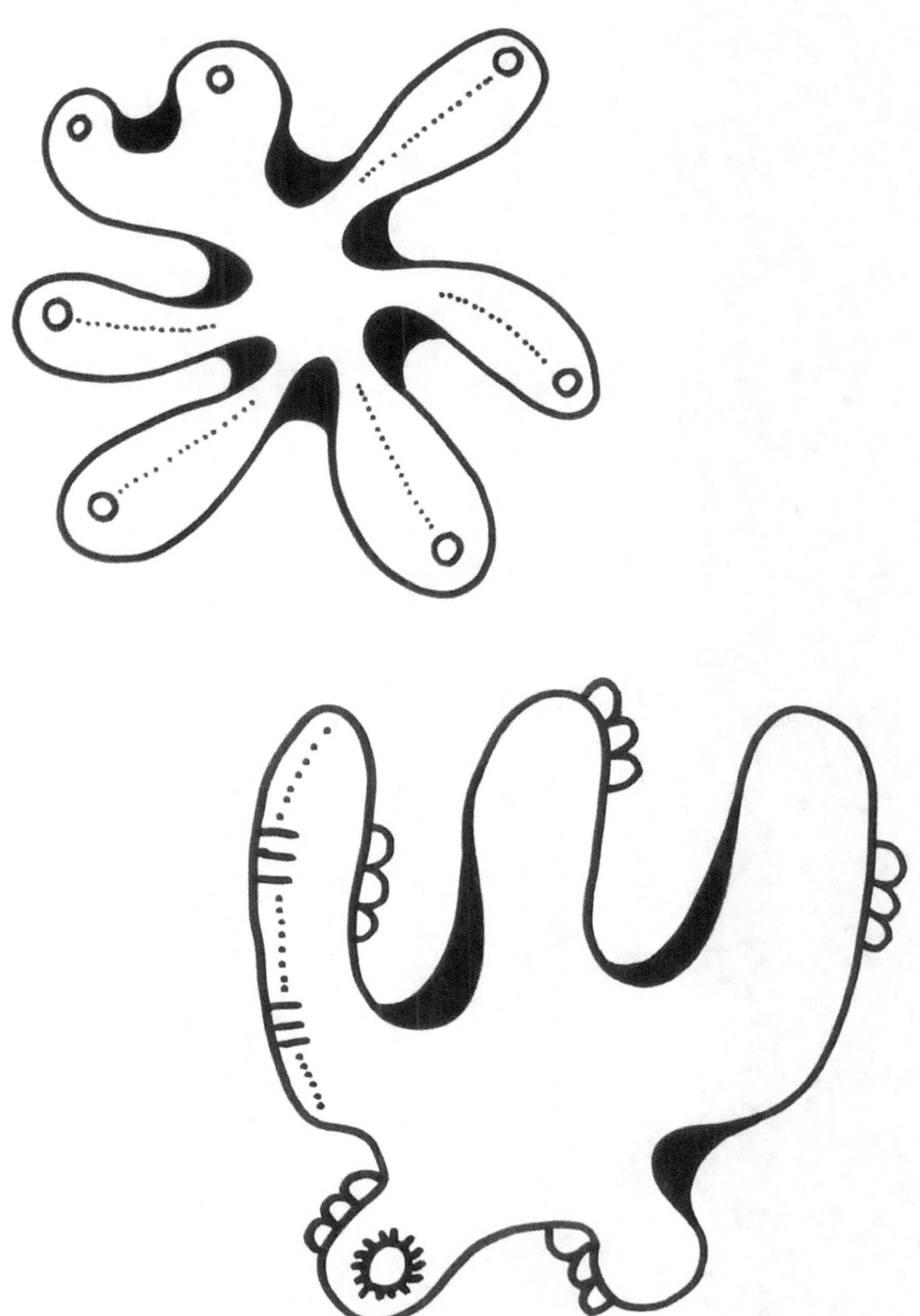

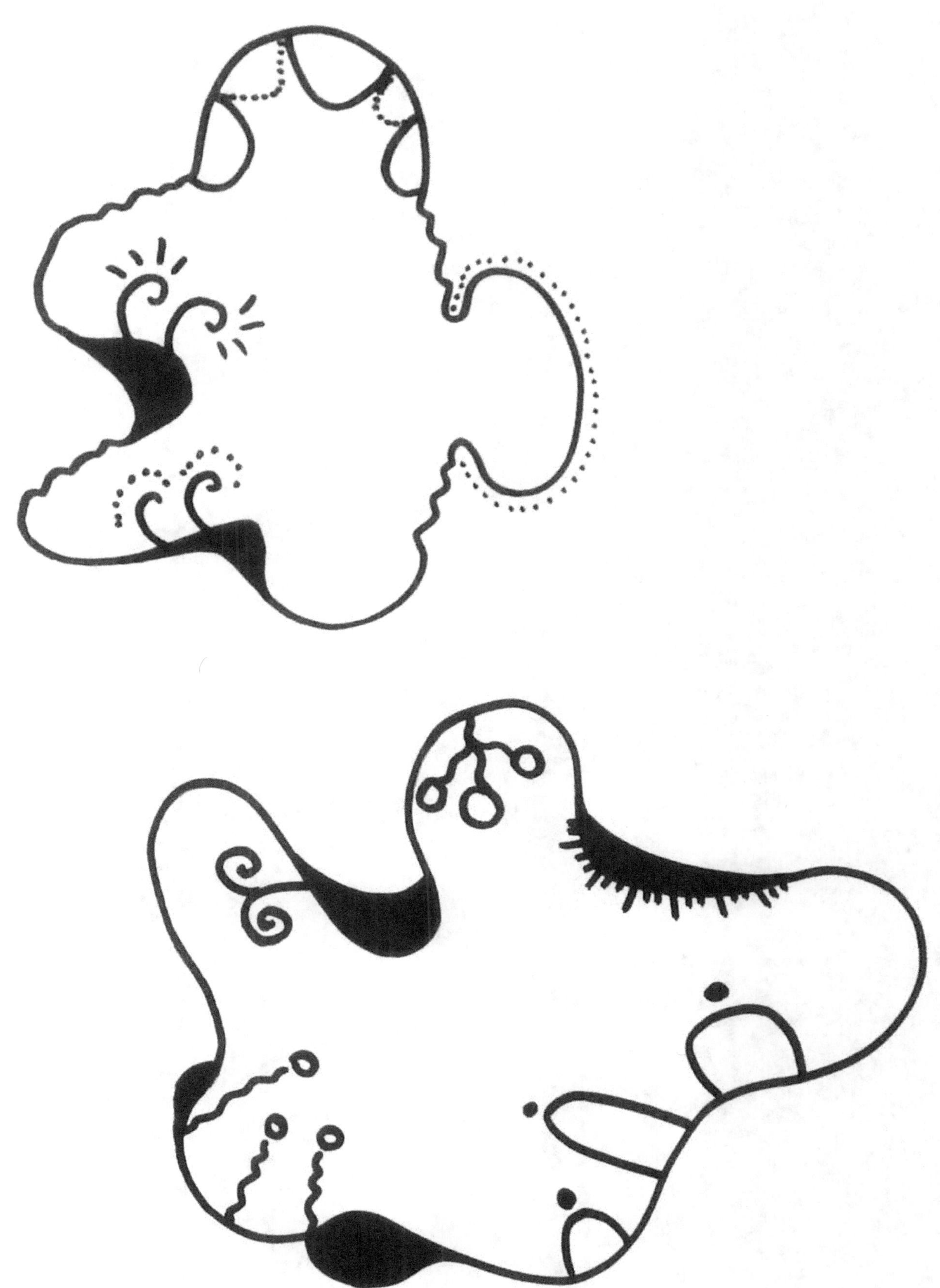

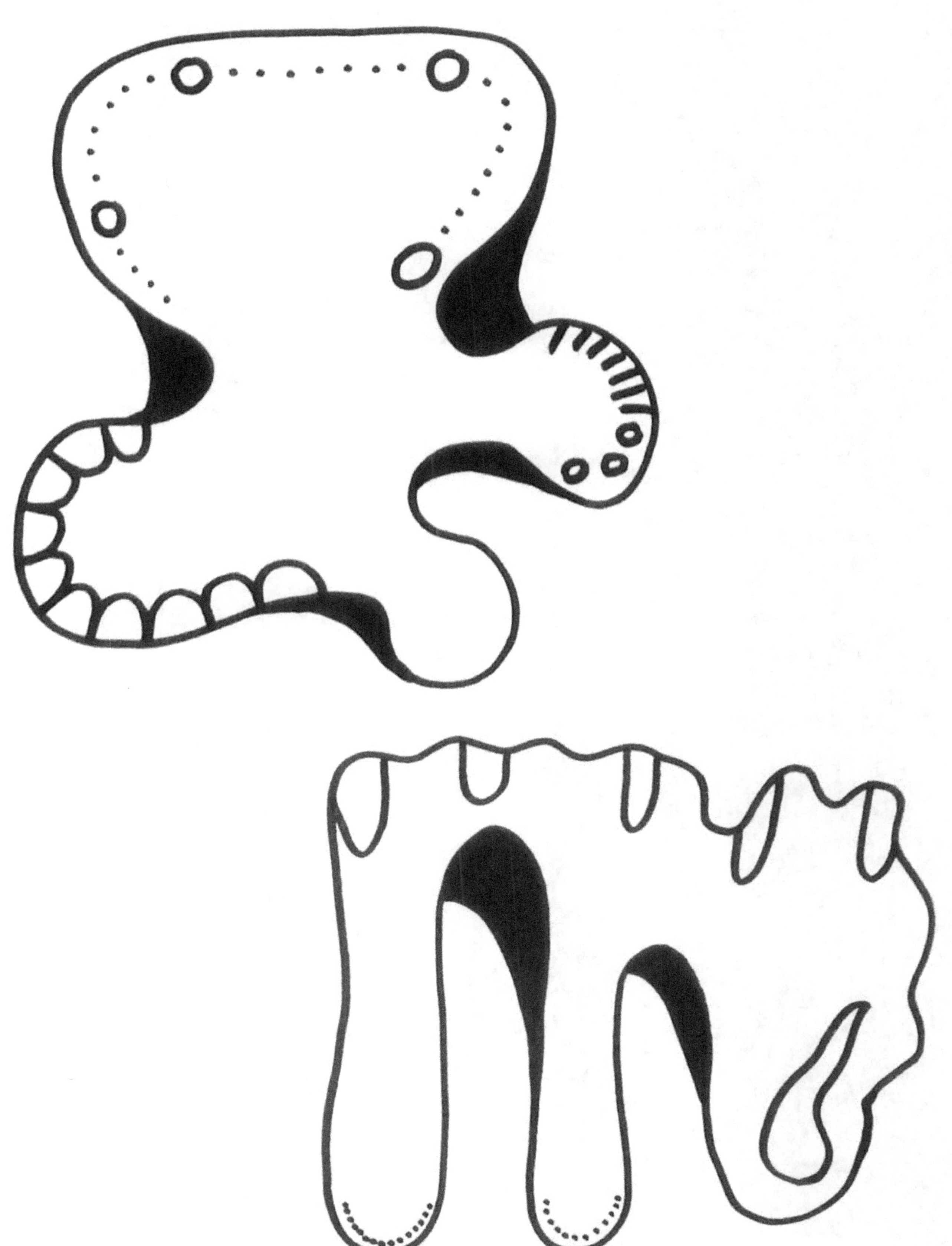